To the Dave Events

Robert Reardon

THE EARLY MORNING LIGHT

A friendly reflection on some of the main
events in the life of the Church of God
reformation movement during
the first fifty years.

By

Robert H. Reardon

Warner Press
Publication Board of the Church of God
Anderson, Indiana

This book is dedicated
with love
and appreciation
to my parents.

Contents

A Personal Foreword

My own association with the Church of God goes back to the year of my birth, 1919, in the Faith Missionary Home, Chicago. My grandmother and her two sisters had been attracted to the home through divine healing literature published by workers in this home. It was here that my mother was saved and "saw the light."

This home, begun in 1895 by Gorham Tufts, grew out of rescue mission work among migrant Germans and Scandinavians pouring into Chicago. In 1898, Mary Cole, a rugged, frontier-type firebrand of a woman preacher, and her brother George arrived on the scene to take up the work. After working out of rented homes for several years, they came by enough money and donated labor to build a more extensive missionary home and chapel at Seventy-fourth and Princeton on Chicago's south side. This was completed in 1903.

To this home many evangelists and itinerant gospel musicians returned between meetings. It was here that plans were laid for evangelistic tours, for street meetings around the city, and for new works among the blacks and immigrants flooding into the factories and steel mills of the area. Pamphlets and tracts came off the small press in the basement and circulated widely from door to door.

No one received a salary. A pattern of communal life, already initiated by the Trumpet Family up in Michigan and over in Moundsville, West Virginia, prevailed. The family ate, worshiped, and prayed together. They exhorted one another, watched each other's conduct, and measured it with care. The discipline was strict. Young "saints" were expected to work hard and to "come under." This was a much-used phrase indicating the need to subject oneself to the disciplines imposed by the spiritual leaders of the home.

Since the Church of God sponsored no Bible schools or colleges in those days, it was to this Chicago home, the first of many such establishments in the church, that my father came in 1899. He had been converted and felt called to the ministry while attending a three-week meeting held by Barney Warren and a "Flying Band of Reformation Saints" at West Liberty, Ohio. My father was shy, of Irish Catholic parents, and had been teaching school for five or six years prior to this experience. He did not get along well at first, had particular trouble being sanctified, and went to the altar twenty-two times.

It was the patience and long-suffering of Mary Cole who held him on his searching path after he reached Chicago. Mary was impulsive, subject to making decisions by dreams, and regularly cast out devils and evil spirits. It was her usual manner to announce that she had direct word on things from above. As time went on, my father began to gain respect and develop his

The Faith Missionary Home on Chicago's south side was completed in 1903.

Mary and George Cole were early leaders at the Missionary Home.

leadership. He was a thoughtful and organized man to whom people turned. His relationship with Mary, though a loving one, often threw off sparks.

George Cole, however, was a warm and encouraging friend. My father tells of entering a season of prayer with Brother George over the unpaid bills, the internal wrangling in the home, and the slowness with which people were wont to accept the Truth. They knelt in prayer and my father reminded the Lord of all his promises and ended his prayer with this urgent command: "We demand immediate results." He recalled feeling Brother George's hand come to rest gently on his head and his voice lifted in prayer: "O God, save this young brother from the sin of immediate results!"

An Early Form of Training

The Chicago home certainly was a creature of the movement's need for training its ministers. These homes sprang up in places like Kansas City, Denver, New York City, and Los Angeles. We had only the apprentice method in operation at that time and a person who was interested in any kind of ministry went to one of the

7

missionary homes and learned by that approach. Eventually several of these homes—ones in New York, Kansas City, Spokane, Denver, and St. Paul Park— became known, at least briefly, as Missionary or Bible Training Schools. If these young people in the homes did well they stayed; if they did not do well they fell by the wayside. It was the sink-or-swim method, the survival of the fittest.

Activities in these centers covered many fronts. Some workers went from door to door with the literature. Others held cottage prayer meetings in various parts of the city. Some held street corner meetings, and others were busy in pastoral work. Some were out praying for the sick. Other activities that were a part of the Chicago home undertaking included a lending library, regular Bible classes, printing and distributing tracts, solicitation for *Gospel Trumpet* subscriptions, and rescue mission provisions for persons who were in destitute circumstances.

The homes were operated entirely by freewill offerings. Each member gave according to ability and received according to need. Most of the congregations that were started in Chicago grew out of efforts from the home.

"Days of Bitter Herbs"

Life in the missionary homes was not plush. Such living without any kind of remuneration required a kind of total dedication few of us know today. Wearing secondhand clothing was common, although at times there was some resistance to this. Once a generous brother brought my father a large black hat, with the comment, "The Lord showed me that I should give this hat to you." My father tried on the hat which came down over his ears and replied, "Thank you very much, but I know the Lord did not tell you to give me this hat." The brother said, "Why not?" My father answered, "Because the Lord knows my size."

Father stuck it out at the home and met and fell in love with my mother, who was a German girl. Germans, you know, save their money, and her parents had been merchants down on Milwaukee Avenue in Chicago. When the word got around that mother was going to marry this young minister who had no salary and wore secondhand clothes and lived in a missionary home, her best friend said, "Well, Pearl, it isn't everyone who can say, 'Blessed be nothing.' "

Of course, their courtship—and even their honeymoon—went on at the home under the watchful eyes of the saints. My mother recalled that right after their marriage she woke up in the middle of the night and saw my father standing in the middle of the bed in his white nightshirt, frantically waving an open umbrella around his head. She said, "I think I've married a crazy man. Eugene, what are you doing?" And he said, "Well, Pearl, it's awfully hot in here. I'm just trying to change the air a little bit."

My father referred to these days as "days of bitter herbs and unleavened bread." Families were crowded close together into restricted quarters, receiving very little financial support and moving in and out to carry the Truth in new and innovative ways. This was not altogether conducive to harmonious living, and a good many tensions developed. Altogether my father spent twenty-two years without a salary in the Faith Missionary Home, traveling widely throughout the community to reach new people and minister to the needy. No neckties were to be worn by the saints, and no wedding rings by the women. So you can imagine the scene when father, with his clerical collar, vest, and black suit, looking every inch like a Roman priest, and my lovely young mother, two children in tow and without a wedding ring, would board the streetcar in the Polish-Catholic neighborhood.

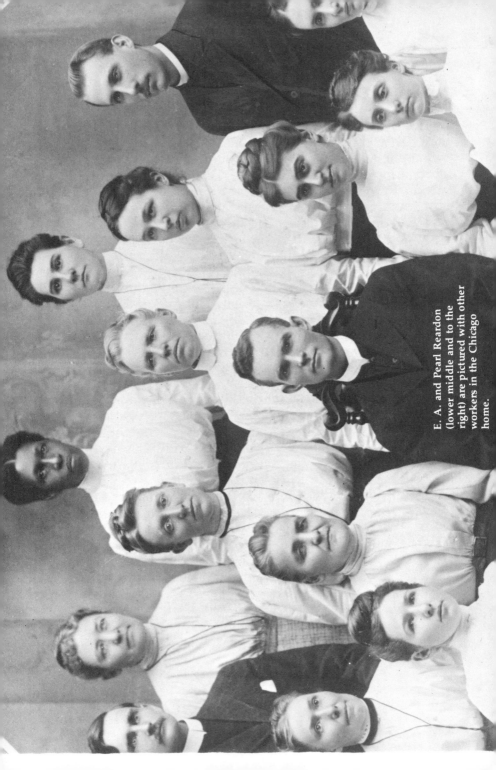

E. A. and Pearl Reardon (lower middle and to the right) are pictured with other workers in the Chicago home.

Growing Up in Anderson

Finally, in the year 1920, our family moved to Anderson and father became the first full-time pastor of Park Place church. Living as a boy and a young man in Anderson, sandwiched around a period in Denver, I knew the leaders of the movement, who were frequent visitors in our home. J. T. Wilson, J. A. Morrison, Russell Olt, E. E. and Noah Byrum, F. G. Smith, C. E. Brown, S. P. Dunn, Nora Hunter, H. M. Riggle, A. T. Rowe, D. O. Teasley, and A. L. Byers came regularly to our house at 914 Walnut Street. Many lived in the community and worshiped with us in the church. I heard them preach and testify, not once but on many occasions. We got to know them well. It is to their credit, and to our advantage, that these nationally-known leaders were passionately committed to a great dream. None of them became rich. All poured their lives, without personal regard, into the bloodstream of the movement.

I have been associated during my entire lifetime with our movement, first as a pastor, and now for thirty-two years as part of the Anderson College faculty and staff. Although some of the things which I say in this discussion may seem unvarnished, as I try to tell the story from the record and as nearly as I know it I shall do it from a heart of great love and appreciation. The persons I have mentioned have been like an extended family; they have shaped my life and everything good that has happened to me. My education, my values, my friends, my opportunities to serve, my wife, the nurture of my family, all the things that I prize above everything else—these things came to me through the life and the work of the Church of God and the people in it.

Chapter 1
Seeking for the Light

When Daniel S. Warner stood up in 1881 among the sparsely populated farmlands around the community of Beaver Dam, Indiana, and declared himself forever free from sects and embraced twice-born believers everywhere, there was every reason for the religious world to yawn. Here was a young maverick, known as a troublemaker by the denomination that had expelled him for holiness preaching at its meeting in Findlay, Ohio. He had little money, no significant organization, only a handful of the faithful to take their stand with him, and part ownership of a holiness paper whose future hung by a thread. There was no radio, no TV, and his message could be heard only as far as he could project his voice and distribute his paper.

Who was this man to whom we owe so much and what was this message that was destined to take hold and prosper in spite of the most trying circumstances?

The main outline of Warner's life has been well chronicled. There remain, however, several aspects of it that hold continual fascination for me and may be worthy of further examination.

No Promising Childhood

Warner's bitter childhood experiences in the home of a tavernkeeper-farmer who was addicted to drink and consequent abuse of wife and family, must have left on the sensitive young lad a mark of pain and insecurity.

Indeed, beatings and abuse were undoubtedly common in this home. Can a child ever erase from memory the sound of drunken voices in the night, the groans and sobbing of a mother being beaten and abused? I think not. It may indeed be that the hostility to drinking still commonly held in the Church of God to this day may well have had its roots in the reformer's early life. In later years he wrote a few sad, poetic lines describing his relationship to his father:

> A mother's heart oppressed with grief, a father's wicked spleen,
> Who cursed his faint and gasping breath, combine to paint the scene.
> He lived, though life was bitter pain, his youth a flood of tears,
> His body doomed to cruel pain, his mind to nervous fears.
> He never knew that *father* was a sweet, endearing name;
> It's very mention was a dread, his life's most deadly bane.
> The demon of intemperance there infused the wrath of hell,
> And most upon *this* sickly head the storm of fury fell.
> O Rum! Thy red infernal flame—I witness to the truth—
> Filled all my mother's cup with pain, and swallowed up my youth.

> —D. S. Warner

The early years of Warner's life will always be shrouded in a certain amount of mystery. Apparently he was a sensitive, asthmatic, but somewhat mischievous lad, growing up, working hard on the farm. Then, to serve in his brother's place, he was inducted into the Union Army in the Civil War as a private in the 195th Ohio Regiment. His experiences in the Civil War were never recorded although I have heard it reported that one night he fell asleep on sentry duty—an unforgivable and hazardous act on the battlefield. After the war was over, Warner returned home to northwestern Ohio and to a period of deep doubting and perplexity in his own life. The post-Civil War period was one of political corruption, social estrangement, and moral decline. The shock of Lincoln's death deeply affected the spirit of the nation.

I have lived these past ten years through a somewhat similar period and know well how easily the young turn from idealism to cynicism, drugs, and despair. Warner's life, however, was dramatically changed through his conversion experience in 1865 at age twenty-three.

A Student at Oberlin

Soon after, he left his school teaching and enrolled in Oberlin College, a school dedicated to learning and labor and passionately committed to abolitionism and coeducation. It was first in the nation to admit women. At one time during the war all faculty were in jail in Elyria for operating an underground railway smuggling slaves into Canada. It is altogether likely that the place of women and blacks in our movement in its early days may have been encouraged by views assimilated by Warner at Oberlin. Here Warner was exposed to persons of culture and refinement, great music for which the school has always been noted, and the excitement of teachers and books.

Dominating the scene at the college was its nationally known evangelist-president, Charles Grandison Finney. While I was a student at Oberlin, I often went to old First church to stand behind Finney's pulpit and imagine, in my mind's eye, young Daniel—twenty-three years of age, sitting out there listening with rapt attention to the nation's foremost preacher and writer of holiness. We have no record that Warner embraced holiness doctrines at the time. We do know that from this time on throughout his life, he was first an evangelist, a herald of the good news that saves people from sin; only second was he a reformer. In no small measure do I attribute this devotion to revivalism to his Oberlin days. It may also be the reason he dropped out of school to become a free-lance, undenominational preacher.

14

Dark Night of the Soul

Two years later, in 1867, he married Tamzen Ann Kerr. This was not Warner's first romance. Earlier he had been caught up in a romance with a Frances Stocking and had become engaged. The affair went sour when Warner began to pray about the matter. He dropped her when he went off to college, and this apparently broke her heart. On the rebound Frances turned to a "rough young man named Boles" whom she married. Sometime later she lost her mind, a matter which troubled Warner deeply, and for which his sensitive heart carried some guilt. Now in 1867 Warner had no inkling of the pain and tragedy about to descend upon him during the next five years. He had met Tamzen while teaching school and had fallen in love with her. After their marriage a son was born who died shortly after birth. Tamzen regained her strength and was soon pregnant again. In 1872 triplet daughters were born. None survived, and the young mother never recovered from the severe complications of this multiple birth. At the end of this tragic year Warner wrote in his diary:

One there was, the dearest of my earthly friends, who a year ago stood by my side. The joy of my life, the sweet innocent object of my fervent love. But she is gone. That dear companion upon whose rosy cheek, and harmless lips I used to impress the kiss of burning, never dying love. O, Tamzen! Thy heart and life, as pure as the white and fleecy snow that this morning covers thy peaceful resting place, has reared an everlasting monument in the hearts of all that knew thee on earth.

—D. S. Warner

It takes little imagination to sense the dark night of the soul through which Warner was passing. The crying out "why" to God, the temptation to bitterness, the grief and

15

D. S. Warner married Tamzen Ann Kerr in 1867.

loneliness—all bring to mind the heart-rending scene of a tender and sensitive young man kneeling alone in the snow, weeping in distress by a fresh grave. This period in his life surely must account for the recurring theme of melancholy which we find threading its way through his writings and hymns. There is something else here, however. Although in later years he carried on the hottest invective against the religious establishment, there was often in his ministry a tenderness with people and a rapport with persons in trouble and pain that drew people to him. Alas, this tenderness did not always characterize those who followed him, nor did it generally characterize his attitude toward those who disagreed with him along doctrinal lines.

16

Preaching in Ohio and Nebraska

After Warner's conversion he felt called into the ministry and associated himself with the Churches of God of North America, sometimes called the Winebrennarians. That group had been formed by John Winebrenner, a German Reformed minister who had been caught up in the revivalism of the early 1800s. The teaching of Winebrenner and his movement had a profound influence on Warner in such matters as the name of the church, Christian unity, and evangelistic outreach. D. S. Warner was licensed to preach by the West Ohio Eldership of the Churches of God in 1872 and was growing rapidly in reputation as a skillful evangelist and pastor. In his first six years of preaching in Ohio and Indiana he spoke 1,241 times, winning 508 souls saved. But his heart turned again to love and in 1874 he married Sarah Keller—she eighteen, he thirty-one—and together they went to the vast, open prairies of Seward, Nebraska, to do home missionary work. In spite of incredible hardship and suffering, Warner managed to service fourteen preaching stations and organize six new congregations. The long separation from home and

In 1874 Warner married eighteen-year-old Sarah Keller and took her to Nebraska.

17

friends, together with Warner's continual absence from their one-room residence, afflicted Sarah with bouts of homesickness. She often wept as Warner set out on one of his long journeys to a preaching point across the plains.

When they returned to pastoral work in Ohio, in 1875, Sarah was great with child. In time a baby girl was born, the apple of Warner's eye. Yet, three years later tragedy struck again. His diary in the year 1878 tells of the death and burial of his darling three-year-old Levilla.

Soon afterwards, Warner's marriage to Sarah seemed to go sour. Its dissolution has been the subject of considerable speculation. It takes little imagination to realize that marriage to an evangelist-reformer was no easy task. In addition to the poverty, there were the frequent shifts from home to home, Sarah's younger age, the humiliation of relying on others for sustenance, the inevitable separations, and Warner's passionate drive to preach and evangelize. There is no question that his work came first, and generally there was little time left for the cultivation of those elements which make for a rewarding marriage relationship. The strain came to a head in 1883 in Bucyrus, Ohio, some years after he had launched out with *The Gospel Trumpet*. A group of fanatics, led by R. S. Stockwell, had convinced Sarah and others of a "third work of grace" in which marital celibacy was a condition of true holiness. Sarah, under the persuasive spell of Stockwell, demanded that Warner sell them the *Gospel Trumpet* publishing work. He refused, and it was not long before she abandoned him and their little son, Sidney. The terrible grief and loneliness which followed nearly drove Warner insane but, with strength from above, he went on with his work. The picture of father and little son traveling to a residential neighborhood in Cincinnati where Sarah had fled, standing outside her house in the rain, begging Sarah to come home—to no avail—is a scene not soon forgotten.

Rejection, Worst Pain of All

It is possible for a man to endure pain, poverty, hunger, and distress. But rejection—to be forsaken—this is the most difficult of all. Warner did not even show up in court to contest the divorce. The charge: desertion. He did not remarry until after Sarah died some years later. Some suspect that the estrangement may have come over extreme views, hinted at in the diaries, which held that sex relations were permissible for Christians only for the purpose of procreation. These are only speculations, and we probably will never know.

After Warner's initial rejection of the doctrine of sanctification, it comes as a surprise to find that in the year 1877 he began to seek this experience. Following a thorough study of the Scriptures, he finally professed the experience of entire sanctification as taught by the Wesleys and others as a second definite cleansing work of grace, and its proclamation became a life long obsession. From this time on, little else was on his mind. This doctrine held a place of preeminence in his preaching and eventually caused his expulsion from the Winebrennarian group. Everywhere Warner went among Church of God congregations, he called people to this second definite work. Many experienced sanctification to the consternation of the Eldership. Warner was not timid in this undertaking. In spite of a first warning and strict prohibitions against preaching and teaching this doctrine, he launched a protracted meeting in the courthouse at Findlay, Ohio, disobeying his warning and invading the territory of Eldership brethren of no mean influence. On January 18, 1878, the standing committee heard charges against him and his license was revoked. He was out!

I have read Warner's account of this affair in his diary. The emotional turbulence it set off can hardly be exaggerated. Families were divided, pastors lined up for and against. Warner was regarded as a troublemaker by some and a martyr by others. Beneath all this, however, we must ask a most serious question. How did Warner handle it? I think he had a hard time with the dissolution of marriage and brotherhood and perhaps never really got over it. It is not easy to be rejected and set aside by your brethren. His later denunciation of sect Babylon and his violent hostility to organization in the church was without doubt fueled by this bitter experience. This rejection, together with his estrangement from Sarah and eventually his break with the Holiness Association in which he had become a rising young preacher and writer, had to affect his emotional life.

Here was this man, frail in health, limited in financial resources, rejected by his denomination, enduring the pain of a marriage come apart, and visited in a few short years by the angel of death. Amazingly this man brought about such an explosion of reformation energy that its influence has been felt around the globe. It is little short of a miracle.

A Fantastic Seventeen Years

After Warner's expulsion from the Eldership in 1878, he entered upon a fantastic period of seventeen brief years which launched and extended the Church of God Reformation movement across the nation. Let us note some of the major sources of energy that inspired and literally drove Warner during this brief period of his life to accomplish his work of heralding the reformation and setting it in motion.

All of Warner's writings provide evidence that he was a lifelong, serious student of the Bible. Persons who wrestle with the Word and begin to follow it, enter into the spirit of reformation which is a constant energizer and purifier in the Church.

To indicate how deeply committed he was we must look again at his own personal covenant with God. It is a masterpiece of personal confession. Walter Horton, one

Warner traveled for a time with this gospel team. He would later marry Frankie Miller (upper right).

of this century's most eminent theologians, was much impressed and moved by it. Obedience to the call of God was total and unconditional. No sacrifice was too great, no burden too heavy.

Warner's personal magnetism and persuasiveness on reformation polemics were legendary. People listened to his scathing denunciations of sects and responded by "coming out." They listened to his call for holiness and flocked to the altar to be sanctified. He was a master persuader. I believe his anger and lashing out at the sects, his inveighing against organization of any kind within the church came from two sources. One was theological. He saw the church as a fellowship of born again and sanctified believers, something which can never be organized by people. The other source is emotional. It was the Eldership, a form of denominationalism, that had rejected him and set him aside. Out of this deep and lasting hurt came emotional power which drove the engine of his anger. Perhaps

21

most pivotal of all, Warner believed his work would herald the gathering of true believers into one body before the end of the age. He believed that he would live to see this happen.

Warner had become a popular writer and leader in the holiness movement as it spread across the country out of its Midwest base. But in a turning point decision which came at the convention of the National Holiness Association in Terre Haute, Indiana, in 1881, Warner withdrew from that organization over what he felt was their support of sectism. According to their bylaws they would work within existing denominations to promote their views. Warner wanted to move beyond sectism in using holiness as a basis for Christian unity free of sectarian structures. It was in this spirit that Warner withdrew from the Association and a few months later made his Beaver Dam declaration.

We know that Warner dipped deeply into the writings of Uriah Smith who had fabricated an elaborate scheme of historical interpretations of the prophetic writings. At first his interest was to refute the Adventists, but the idea that current events and predictions could be made from these prophetic writings proved to be of irresistible fascination. In the early 1890s, articles along this line began to appear, and there emerged a scheme of identifying the movement in prophetic forecasting. One day Warner shook himself awake and said, "this is it!" What will make a man leave home and kindred, suffer persecution, endure pain and humiliation, and press on in spite of all odds?

I think there was a moment, heavy with destiny, when Warner felt in his heart that God, in the year 1880, was breaking again into history; that it was foretold by the prophets; and that Warner was a central figure, being used of God to usher in the last phase of history before the end of the age. It was this same sense of urgency that also drove his associates in what has been called a "flying ministry" of planting the reformation banners across the nation and, soon, the world.

Chapter 2
Building in the Light

When Warner died in 1895, the burden of leadership fell on the shoulders of a young man by the name of E. E. Byrum. To understand the significance of this young man in our history we are well advised to assess the situation at Warner's death. In 1879, sixteen years before his death, Warner bought a half-interest in a holiness paper, *The Herald of Gospel Freedom*, for $250. It was sponsored by the rebellious Eldership of Northern Indiana, and owned by I. W. Lowman. There can be little doubt that the disaffection of the Northern Indiana Eldership was caused in some considerable measure by Warner's preaching and teaching as he traveled this territory, carrying the banner of holiness and crying out against the evils of lodges and secret societies. And so, when he was expelled and his license lifted, he fled to northern Indiana and his friends.

By 1880 his name appeared as sole editor and the same year the paper was merged with a holiness paper published in Indianapolis and called *The Pilgrim*. The new publishing venture was named *The Gospel Trumpet*. The first two issues came out in the northern Indiana community of Rome City, and then Warner moved down to Indianapolis in abject poverty to form a new partnership. There the kitchen of his house became the scene of the publishing work. Later, always skirting on the edge of bankruptcy, the fragile little magazine would move on to Cardington and Bucyrus, Ohio, Williamston, and then Grand Junction, Michigan—six locations in six years!

By an unusual set of circumstances, *The Gospel Trumpet* played a pivotal role in the Church of God movement unique in American church history. It was the *Trumpet* that set the standard, that heralded reformation imperatives, that was advisor and counselor. The *Trumpet* helped the scattered saints to find each other, brought news of great revivals and victories, and shared prayer requests for healing. It was the rallying force, the visible instrument. Its editor kept a list of subscribing saints—subscribers only, not church members. During this heralding period it was Warner who was prophet, teacher, evangelizer, poet, advisor, theologian—the *voice* of the reformation. Since *The Gospel Trumpet* was the only formal organizational entity, it was Warner's dominant personality and the *Trumpet* that kept the movement from disintegrating into a thousand isolated and disconnected parts.

A Farm Boy from Indiana

At this critical time, young Enoch Byrum appeared on the scene. He was the seventh of thirteen children in a prosperous Indiana farm family with Quaker and United Brethren rootage that had homesteaded in Randolph County, seven miles northwest of Union City. He grew up in the rigors of mid-nineteenth century farm life—into the fields at sunup, out at sundown. His father was one of the founders of Ridgeville College, the first of several colleges Enoch attended for short periods of time. He later went on to Eastern Indiana Normal School (now Ball State University), Otterbein College, and what is now Valparaiso University. It was the practice of Byrum's father to endow his children with farms of their own upon coming of age, a factor of affluence not to be forgotten in the unfolding of events. Byrum came home from college in his early twenties to find the Prospect Chapel United Brethren Church torn apart. His mother and his brother Fletcher had been "sanctified and had

24

come out of sectism in a protracted meeting held by the saints." Soon Byrum's heart began to beat and his blood began to stir at the reformation call, and he followed this lead. At his first camp meeting in Bangor, Michigan, Byrum was introduced to Warner by Henry Wickersham, one of Byrum's cousins, and a plan began to emerge to save the *Trumpet* which was now wracked with internal financial and other problems.

A Modest Operation Indeed

The *Trumpet* was a limited undertaking during those days. The entire holdings had been moved to Grand Junction, Michigan, in a single boxcar and moved into an 800-square-foot abandoned store. Warner was on the road much of the time, Brother Michels was a silent partner, and the third owner, J. C. Fisher, was having an extra-marital love affair and planning to divorce his wife. It was a time of considerable tension. Warner could not reconcile his continued association with Fisher in publishing a holiness paper managed by a person so obviously out of harmony with the sanctified life. Fisher did not want out and came forward with an impossibly high offer of a thousand dollars to sell his one-third interest. But Warner agreed, not knowing where he would get the money.

It was at this point that Warner met the twenty-six-year-old Byrum. That young man was newly sanctified, newly "come out," attending his first camp meeting, untrained in doctrine, unknown among the saints, foreign to any kind of publishing business management, but he made a decision which was one of the pivotal turning points in our history as a people. It was young Byrum who came forward with his inheritance to buy out Fisher. Ultimately he, with his younger brother, Noah, at Warner's death, came to own the Trumpet Company.

Enoch Byrum (second from left) with other ministers (H. M. Riggle, right).

When Byrum took over management, he really took over. He moved to Grand Junction, Michigan, the next day after the agreement was consummated. Young Byrum had exactly ten days to learn the ropes before Warner left for an evangelistic tour that kept him absent from the office for ten months. During this time, Byrum was publisher, business manager, managing editor, and overseer of every facet of the office. Field reports had to be carefully screened to keep out the wolves in sheep's clothing. Articles had to be examined for doctrinal regularity with imposters on every hand.

But after eleven years at the job, Byrum had put together a company of one hundred people. By 1895, the year of Warner's death, Byrum was mailing out seventy-five hundred copies of *The Gospel Trumpet* each week and had attracted more that three thousand subscribers. That same year he had increased annual volume in literature, tracts, songbooks, and other material to more than two million pieces. Some record for a neophyte in the publishing business! E. E. Byrum stayed firmly at the helm for the next three decades, riding out storm after storm, making bold new moves, and exercising an impact on the growth and shape of the movement unequaled by any other man.

Enoch had early been joined by his brother Noah as a partner in the publishing work. Just before Warner's death the three partners set up an agreement providing that none of the partners would ever get any personal profit out of the enterprise. If one would withdraw, he would get only the exact amount he put into it. Noah remained as treasures into the 1940s. I remember him very well; when someone would raise a financial question, Noah would say in his high, nasal voice, "Well, brethren, there's the figgers!" And there wasn't much else you could say.

The stories have it that it was Noah who discovered an interesting thing that had a lot to do with the publishing work moving from Grand Junction to Moundsville, West Virginia. In Grand Junction they were paying from three to six dollars a ton for coal to fire the boilers, but at Moundsville, near the coal mines, it could be delivered for as little as thirty-five cents a ton. So they loaded up the Trumpet people and their belongings into two passenger coaches, nine freight cars, and one baggage car, and headed for Moundsville.

A School on the Way?

Before he died, Warner was contemplating the establishment of a school. It is not altogether clear what he had in mind. We do know that missionaries and gospel workers who could not qualify as residents in Grand Junction had trouble getting their children into the county schools. A school was established for these children in Grand Junction, and it appears that Warner contemplated expanding it into a training school in 1895. The first meeting to lay plans was called but never came about, because Warner fell ill. One week later he died. Shortly thereafter Byrum, in response to a letter from the field, flatly stated that there was no school nor did they intend to have one.

Wide-Ranging Contributions

I should like to expand somewhat on the influence of E. E. Byrum, this remarkable man who started out seemingly so ill-equipped for the job. As I reflect on his ministry among us, several major contributions stand out.

1. *He saved the Trumpet* and forged it into a powerful, cohesive influence. Subsequent inquiries into the affairs of the company indicate beyond a shadow of a doubt that neither he nor Noah prospered personally from the phenomenal growth of the company. They put in their time freely and brought the company through two major moves and reorganization as an institution totally owned and controlled by the church.

2. *It was Byrum who organized the family commune-type system* in the company. Later, when the missionary homes were organized, they followed the same fundamental concept. No one profited. The resources went to further the reformation message. No salaries were paid. The work relied on freewill offerings and the sale of books and tracts. With free labor, without executive salaries and dividends to pay, with the growing sale of literature, the influx of donations, the tax-free status, and the level of sacrifice expected, it is not difficult to see why the company mushroomed at a fantastic rate. When Byrum brought his troops from Moundsville to Anderson in 1906, it took a whole train (twenty-eight cars) to move the community.

The work was moved to Anderson because of the greater centrality to our developing church population, the availability of good land at a give-away price as the Anderson gas boom waned, and the immediate access to good rail transportation. It is a well-known story how Noah and Enoch Byrum arrived on the scene in 1905, got off the old interurban at Third and College, crawled under the farm fence, and walked the acreage now occupied by our national work. They liked it as a site, knelt down in a clearing, and dedicated it there and then, without title of any kind, to Almighty God and his church. Soon timbers were coming in gondola cars from the now-closed St. Louis Exposition buildings. Blocks were being made by hand, and the saints were at work erecting the publishing office and plant, an old peoples' home, and other buildings to house the community. That first major building they put up was a big residence where all the Trumpet workers and their families would live. It was a building of some forty-two thousand square feet and included kitchen, dining area, and living space for all the workers who gave their services without pay. It would later become the main building of Anderson College, standing at Fifth and College Drive until replaced by the present Decker Hall.

3. *He wrote.* Byrum will not be counted one of the scholars of the movement. He did not have a classical education, was not disposed to scholarly pursuits, and tended to be some what parochial. *But he wrote.* It could be assumed that as owner and publisher he had something to do with the eighteen books put out over his name. In addition to his editorials, these books traveled far and wide establishing his office as the standard of authority in doctrine and purity.

Noah and Enoch Byrum engineered the move to Anderson where this home for Trumpet workers (later Old Main at Anderson College) was erected.

N. H. Byrum works at his desk at Gospel Trumpet Company. Kate Hamblin (later, Mrs. Oscar Flynt) is at left.

4. *He ruled.* As Russell Byrum put it to me with a chuckle, Uncle Enoch owned the church. There was only one roster of the saints—*The Gospel Trumpet* subscription list—and he alone had access to it, to know who they were, and where. It was Byrum who wrote, screened, and published "the Truth once delivered to the saints." It was Byrum who adjudicated Trumpet family disputes. It was Byrum who decided who came into the Trumpet Home and who went out.

It was Byrum who had to deal sharply with the young Turks who came charging into Moundsville demanding that their anti-cleansing views be heard. They were finally heard in a public meeting, their arguments "struck down with biblical proofs," and they were left with no margin of compromise. Byrum felt that to compromise would be to bring the entire reformation crashing to the ground. The saints to whom God had revealed his truth could hardly admit to error. The anti-cleansers departed and, according to C. E. Brown, took with them at least half of the most promising leadership of the movement. A sad day, indeed!

5. *He was visible.* E. E. Byrum was of medium height, portly, with a stolid, unsmiling visage. He was straight as a ramrod and leaned slightly backward when he walked. When he entered the room there was an unmistakable air of authority about him. He was always on serious business. Faithfulness and hard work were his watchwords. He traveled widely throughout the church and early in the century traveled abroad, investigating the ancient manuscripts at the British Museums in London and the Vatican Library regarding the faith-healing passages. He stayed in the homes of hundreds of saints across the continent. Everywhere a kind of awe and respect were accorded him.

I often sat near him in Park Place church during prayer meeting, and the Byrums—Lucena being his third wife—were in our home many times. Byrum was known in our neighborhood as a somewhat erratic driver, holding the wheel stiff-armed as though reining in a team of obstinate horses. The most dangerous interurban crossing in Anderson was always the corner of Third and College, near the Byrum home on the site now occupied by the Anderson College Library. As the trains approached, the motorman gave forth a blast on his horn that would wake the dead. This intimidated Enoch Byrum not in the least. Beginning at least a block in advance, he leaned on his own horn. Looking neither right nor left and trusting in God's providence, he plunged across the tracks. Luckily he was never done in.

Despite the fact that Byrum spoke with a slight lisp and in a fairly monotonous tone, it did not keep him from moving back and forth across the church in homes, camp meetings, and revivals where his strong, stabilizing influence held the movement together. And, when the occasion called for it, he could resolve a hot issue in a remarkable way. From 1908 to 1914 there developed heated debates over the wearing of neckties. Some were red hot for wearing a tie. Others regarded it as a worldly "superfluity." The battle was waged in ministers' meetings and camp meetings with such heat that threats were sounded by the radical brethren to start a new paper, get a new editor, and publish anti-compromising literature if a clear stand were not taken. Byrum, conservative on the issue at first, began to moderate his position and wrote September 11, 1913, in the *Trumpet*:

> The Trumpet has no disposition to swerve to the right or to the left in order to get on the radical or on the liberal side, but prefers to *stand on the Lord's side* on all questions at all times. . . . So far as the dress question is concerned, The Trumpet has always advocated and shall continue to advocate, plainness of dress.

Not satisfied, the radicals—including Willis Brown and N. S. Duncan—did pull off and start a paper called *The Herald of Truth*. Descendants of this group still carry on their work today in Guthrie, Oklahoma. Fortunately, Brown and Duncan came back.

But the question would not die in Indiana, and Byrum was called to the Yellow Lake Camp Meeting to settle the issue once and for all. The tension built to a fever pitch as Byrum gathered himself to preach in the evening service. Seated within arm's length at the right of the pulpit was the old gospel warrior, M. P. Rimmer, holding on his lap a ten-gallon hat with a bright red ribbon as a hatband. Before saying a word, Byrum reached down, lifted the hat from Rimmer's lap, took off the hatband, and lowered it over his head so that the bow came to rest where a necktie would be. Byrum stood there in silence for all to take the lesson in. They got the point. Nothing was ever said about neckties after that.

It is interesting to observe that men fared much better than women on the dress question. Except for the wedding ring and the necktie as outward manifestations of resident carnality, there were few other prohibitions for men. The women, however, did not fare so well. Mary Cole wrote:

Not long after I was sanctified I received my first light on the subject of dress. One Sunday morning, while listening to a sermon, a voice began to talk to my soul; "You profess to be sanctified, living a holy life, and yet your headdress shows conformity with the world." Sunday after Sunday the same still small voice talked to me this way. Finally, I said, "I shall not allow my conscience to be tortured in this way any more." Early Monday morning I took the flowers off my hat. As I did so, the voice of God said, "Put those flowers in the fire." I immediately obeyed and from that day to this I have never been tempted to restore the flowers to my hat.

Few persons did more to rule the women of the Church of God than Sister C. E. Byers of Springfield. Coming out of a Mennonite background it was she who set the standards of plainness of dress in Springfield, thence throughout Ohio, and from there to the farthest corners of the church. It was the shapeless dress, without ornamentation of pins or jewelry of any kind, that satisfied requirements. No wedding bands, long, uncut hair braided and done up on top of the head, no make-up (a wicked practice of "painted women" and harlots)—these were the marks of sanctified, holy, reformation women.

As far as social practices among the young was concerned, the road was strict, indeed. In his book *To Men and Boys*, off the Trumpet press in 1905, D. O. Teasley wrote about courtship:

My idea of genuine courtship is for those who are intending matrimony, or those who might have any idea that they might unite in marriage, to sit at a reasonable distance from each other, look each other squarely in the face, and talk business. Above all, shun a giddy, funny, proud, fashion-loving woman, for she will make you ashamed, run you into debt, and let your house and children go to ruin. All kissing, fondling, and caressing should be left out of courtship, at least until after engagement, then indulged in very sparingly.

What a miracle it was that any of our parents ever made it to the marriage altar!

Even the children came in for strict guidance. In a question-and-answer column in *The Gospel Trumpet* in 1906:

There may be a few innocent games for the smaller children that are so full of play, but care should be used to avoid such games that create evil, feed a spirit of ambition, and such indeed as do not stop with boys and girls but are played in gambling circles or houses of ill-fame. The larger children do not need much play. Under proper training, children, also young people, may be very profitably entertained at home by musical exercises and by teaching, walking exercises for recreation, and by Sunday school and Bible reading. Aside from these occasionally a stroll off for fishing and so forth are more safe with a guardian than are games of modern invention.

6. *Healing was his favorite theme.* I have referred previously to the reverence and awe accorded Enoch Byrum wherever he appeared. Although his authority sprang directly from his position as editor, his mystique grew out of his gift of healing. This gift sprang from one of the most deeply moving experiences of his life. While still on the farm, he watched a favorite sister become ill and die with tuberculosis. Before many weeks he came to

realize he was also infected. After consulting several physicians he concluded that unless there was help from a higher source, he had little hope of surviving. In desperation, he turned to the New Testament, read again the great faith passages, and in his own words:

> Not knowing how to pray the prayer of faith I knelt alone in my room and talked to the Lord as I would have talked to a friend and told him that I believed his Word and that he could heal me. Then and there I placed my case in his hands to heal me, and I believed he would do it.

I have heard and offered many prayers for divine healing. I have heard preachers shout, command, exhort, as though God were afar off. I often heard Byrum pray for the sick. It always was a calm, sometimes matter-of-fact, friendly conversation with God, simply claiming his promises. We can never underestimate the role of divine healing among us. Pastors were called in times of sickness. Religious meetings were places where signs and wonders took place. It was the presence of healing miracles that drew thousands into the movement: the accounts of these healings were the most exciting parts of the *Trumpet*. This doctrine of healing was placed squarely in the doctrine of the Atonement and was thus understood to be as much a part of the good news as salvation from sin. Divine healing attracted masses of people and gave authenticity to the reformation movement.

Shortly before Warner died in 1895, Byrum began to feel this special burden for healing and to sense that God was endowing him with this gift. With some misgivings about laying claim to such a divine gift, Byrum went to Warner to seek counsel. After hearing him out, Warner placed his hands on Byrum's head, announced, "Brother Byrum, this is of God," and offered a prayer of thankfulness and blessing. The emphasis set in motion at that moment can never be overestimated.

Being a practical man, Byrum soon worked out his approach to healing:

(a) Healing is a part of our spiritual birthright along with salvation from sin, and sanctification.

(b) Healing comes contractually, one might say automatically, when the conditions are right. That is, one must clear away any sinful impediments of attitude, renounce any reliance on man-made remedies; call for the laying on of hands and anointment with oil, accept the promises of God and claim victory.

There can be no doubt from the record that miracles did happen. After leaving the editorship, Byrum traveled far and wide carrying on his ministry of healing. His anointed handkerchiefs were sent into hundreds of homes and his quarters in the Gospel Trumpet office were filled with the crutches, canes, orthopedic devices, and other evidences of healing.

There can be no doubt as well that for many years the contract method did much harm, and the doctrine of healing was twisted into some grotesque forms. Can one imagine the guilt which lay for a lifetime on C. W. Naylor? He was never healed, and yet from his bed poured out such tender books of helpfulness as *The Secret of the Singing Heart* and some of our most beautiful hymns. Byrum said, "Naylor would have been healed but he never *claimed* his healing."

My wife's mother was dying of a kidney ailment in Princeton, Indiana, and had followed the urging of the local congregation to trust God completely and to demonstrate this faith by refusing the ministration of a physician. It was strongly felt among the saints at Princeton that God's power and might would be

In later years E. E. Byrum conducted a world-wide divine healing ministry.

demonstrated and the reformation witness would be plainly validated in the town, when this lovely and well-known woman was healed. After E. E. Byrum's visit she claimed healing, rose from her bed, and appeared in church amid a great emotional outburst of shouting and rejoicing. In a few days a relapse came and she was gone. Neighbors could never forget the bitterness they felt toward her husband for not seeking medical advice and care. That was a hard Christmas for Vernor B. Hurst and those three small children.

My father was E. E. Byrum's pastor for the last ten years of his life and ministered to him as he lay dying at the ripe age of eighty-one. Even in these evening years of his life Enoch could not reconcile his illness with what he had taught. It was on his mind, so father said, to the end.

He Brought Order and Cohesion

Although there may have been flaws of humanness in his character, E. E. Byrum must remain a central personality in our history. Warner may have been the reformer, the herald, and the energizer; but it was Byrum who managed to bring order, form, and cohesion to the great burst of reformation energy literally exploding during this time. When he stepped down as editor in 1916, it was the end of an era. The movement was coming on in numbers. Younger leaders were beginning to feel their strength and to demand their place in the sun. When Byrum laid down his pen as editor and the Trumpet Company was brought into our general work as a corporation wholly accountable to the General Ministerial Assembly, no man—not even his successor—wielded such pervasive influence in the life of the church.

At this juncture in our history, two events took place which were destined to shake the movement to its very foundations. Not long after F. G. Smith was installed as the new editor in chief, J. T. Wilson set in motion a tiny educational venture as a department of the company. By all odds, the single most significant struggle in the movement was soon set up, but when the smoke cleared away the back of fanaticism, cultism, and the power of theological authority held by the editor was finally broken. Thank God, in whose providence it happened! Thank God for F. G. Smith and John Morrison whose love for the church was greater at last than their differences! But that is another story.

Chapter 3
Leading and the Light

When E. E. Byrum put down his pen in 1916, the Church of God reformation movement was growing by leaps and bounds. The Gospel Trumpet Company with its dedicated workers was sending forth the reformation message in songs, tracts, books, and periodicals. Congregations were being raised up in homes, storefronts, and abandoned church buildings. The supply of ministers was no great problem, for eagerness to serve ran high and no formal education was either available or required. In reply to a question regarding credentials, D. S. Warner once wrote in the *Trumpet* that the only credentials required for the ministry were "to be filled with the Holy Spirit and have a reasonable knowledge of the English language." Both men and women stepped forward to give leadership to the saints and to exercise the pastoral function. As new saints poured into the movement, they brought many of their old ideas and ways along. Some of these ideas began to tear apart the fabric of the movement. One man, more perhaps than any other, gave a strong skeletal structure to our faith and practice. His name: F. G. Smith.

Stepping into the Light

Frederick George Smith was born on a farm near Lacota, Michigan, on November 12, 1880. His parents were earnest and devout Christians, deeply involved in the life of the Methodist Church. When Samuel Speck and Sebastian Michels came to town in 1883 preaching reformation ideas, the Smiths stepped out into the "light" and took their stand for the "Truth." From this time on the Smith farmhouse became a regular stopping point for musicians and evangelists. It was in this setting that young Freddy imbibed deeply of reformation ideas and songs. In 1883 the Smiths traveled to their first camp meeting at Bangor, Michigan. At this meeting a number of spectacular healings took place which influenced Fred greatly. In the fall of 1890, at a protracted meeting near his home conducted by D. S. Warner, the boy gave his heart to God. Warner knelt by his side, little realizing the central role that this young convert would someday play.

A little later it was Smith's ability at shorthand, self-taught, that brought him to the attention of E. E. Byrum. So it was that in 1897 he went to work for the Gospel Trumpet Company, a lad of seventeen, with little formal education. Before long he became Byrum's private secretary. A year later he was preaching, and by 1900 he was out in evangelistic work. When the Trumpet family moved to Moundsville, Fred was invited to live with William G. Schell, whose preoccupation with prophetic writings had led him to regard D. S. Warner as a special instrument of God. Schell was a visionary, an idealist who leaned toward sensationalism, socialism, and a modified episcopal organization. Under E. E. Byrum's watchful eye he didn't last long with these views and was soon raising sugar beets in the Northwest to make a living.

Catapulted to Prominence

Stimulated by Schell's initial encouragement, young Smith's bright mind was at work. He put the finishing touches on his first manuscript in 1906, and it was published in 1908 under the title *The Revelation Explained*. The writing of this book immediately catapulted Smith into national prominence in the movement as its ablest

By twenty F. G. Smith had been E. E. Byrum's private secretary and had entered evangelistic work.

authority on church history and biblical interpretation at age twenty-eight. The book was essentially an expression of the ideas propounded by Warner and others, but it expanded these views with great skill and conviction. If one accepted Smith's reading of the apocalypse, there unfolded in his chart of sacred history a grand design, culminating in the year 1880. At that time God was not simply bringing another religious group into being but was actually bringing forth a mighty reformation destined to sweep across the world and to gather into one fold all true, born-again believers before the final culmination of the end of time. The book gave the new, struggling, disinherited, unrecognized movement a divine unction and identity akin to the chosen people of Israel. It became one of the pillars in the house of our standard literature.

At this time there came an urgent plea that would play an important part in Smith's life. In the summer of 1912, at the urging of G. P. Tasker, F. G. agreed to go to Syria to preach and evangelize. He and his wife, Birdie, arrived in Beirut on September 4, 1912. It was here that Smith conceived the idea of writing a primer for young

Lebanese converts. Much of it was written in 1913, in the mountains above Beirut where many of the city dwellers regularly repaired to avoid the summer heat. This book was completed by the time he left to return to the States and was published under the title, *What the Bible Teaches.*

The book was an instant success, went through several printings, and sold more that 100,000 copies. It made him, by all accounts, the principal voice of the movement while still in his early thirties. In a period of rapid expansion the book gave the movement a theological spine which welded us together. As time went on it became a standard source of doctrine, the centerpiece of every church library, and the esteemed possession of almost every saint's home. In time it became the primer for every candidate for ordination and the standard of orthodoxy by which he or she was judged. A few years ago, his wife Birdie Smith, then in her nineties and still living in a nursing home in Anderson, was asked what advice she might have for a young minister. She threw her head back in a delightful laugh and said, "Tell him to buy a copy of *What the Bible Teaches.*"

Even in a current reading, the book's language is clean and persuasive, its arguments and exposition put forward in an easily understood and compelling way. It will probably never be surpassed in popularity nor in influence within the Church of God. Unfortunately, it came to have authority nearly akin to the Scriptures themselves. This brought such great influence to the author that when it was time for E. E. Byrum to lay down the burdens of his editorial office, it was F. G. Smith who had won the right to sit in his place. At age thirty-five, in the year 1916, his name first appeared on the masthead of *The Gospel Trumpet* of June 15. He held this office for the next fourteen years, writing principally in the areas of missions and the church. I cannot overemphasize the sincere devotion and leadership abilities exercised by F. G. Smith during his tenure.

William Ebel (above) baptized L. H. Morgan in the baptismal pool on the Anderson campgrounds. Gospel Trumpet Company board members posed for this picture (below) about the time F. G. Smith became editor in chief. Smith is second from left, top row.

43

F. G. Smith was a short, stocky, powerfully built man. He was not given to frivolous conversation or small talk. He had an intense look, seemed rarely to relax, and was held in fear, admiration, and awe by his brethren. His ability to sense the mood of the church was uncanny. His preaching style was like a carefully prepared legal brief, moving along from point to point, supported always by Scripture.

I can recall hearing him in the old tabernacle at camp meeting time, restrained in delivery, but coming on and warming to his subject. He was like a tightly wound steel spring. When he came to the climax he would move into a few short jumps which released the pent-up emotions of the audience in an awesome way. Some people wept, others shouted, and some ran up and down the aisles praising the Lord. It was a scene to be pondered by students of psychology, and feared by any detractors who might be present.

Opposing Human Organization

Brother Smith warned often about the dangers of organization. When the saints of German extraction in Michigan, inspired by the propensities of their ancestors to organize, decided to organize a state assembly, he summoned them to Anderson to inquire what this madness was all about. Did they intend to organize along sect lines? God forbid! They soon "came under." Smith's view was straightforward. The "charismatic" process— the endowment of gifts—was the prerogative of the Holy Spirit alone, who appointed and placed the servants of the church. Brother Smith felt that his position of leadership was ordained by God, that his writings were at the direction of and carried insights given by the Holy Spirit. He felt that whatever authority he exercised came from the same source. A great portion of the reformation movement looked to Smith as their leader, champion, and guide. Consequently, what he said and wrote was to them the law and the gospel.

Lowrey Quinn, for fifty years one of our leading pastors, told me about going one day as a student at the Bible Training School, over to the Trumpet office to call on F. G. Smith. "What advice do you have for a young man? How did you come to your place of responsibility?" he asked.

Smith replied, "I got in line and I stayed in line."

The Impulse to Democracy

At this time, however, a powerful impulse was beginning to form in the church, the national impulse toward democracy. A great war was being fought to make the world safe for its exercise, so said President Wilson. This impulse, so deep in the lives of the American people, could not be walled out of the church. In 1917 when the General Ministerial Assembly was organized, the door to spiritual democracy was sprung open and things were never the same in the church after that. Hereafter, disputes were adjudicated elsewhere than in the editor's office, and elections to positions of responsibility were made more often by the democratic process. New organisms to serve the church were established, accountable to the Assembly rather than as departments of the Gospel Trumpet Company. Smith viewed this with some alarm and continued to caution against ecclesiastical control of the life of the church in his editorials.

A School Is Born

It was the birth of the Bible Training School in 1917, under the urging of J. T. Wilson and Russell Byrum, that was to give F. G. Smith his greatest concern. Even so, the soil for a school was not promising. Reformation polemics had labeled DDs as "dumb dogs," poured

Students and faculty of the young Anderson Bible Training School gathered for this picture in 1919. Founder J. T. Wilson stands at right. Faculty is seated along the front row. Future President John A. Morrison is fifth from left.

contempt on the sterility of seminaries, and eyed the entire religious education establishment with suspicion. It was a pure, reborn church led by the Holy Spirit that would gather the saints into *one body* at the end of the age. The sects, now gasping out their last breath, were regarded as being presided over by hireling pastors whose credentials were humanly-made and therefore false. Their seminaries, devoid of truth, were creatures doomed to decay and obsolesence. It was the blind leading the blind.

In 1917, last reformationism was at its zenith with its predictions of the imminent end of the age. The church was on the march, growing rapidly. Neither E. E. Byrum nor F. G. Smith used his position to launch the school. Publicly and privately, both urged against such an endeavor. It was assumed that the apprentice method of training ministers in the missionary homes and in churches under guidance of experienced pastors was sufficient.

The polarities were soon sharply drawn between the few who longed for an educational program and those opposed. One side held that education was primarily to train and indoctrinate. The other side saw it as learning and the broad cultivation of the mind. One side held that the Truth had once been delivered to the saints, revealed, packaged, printed, and has only to be proclaimed. Its object was to give answers. The other side held that questions were appropriate, that the nature of Truth was dynamic, and that its purpose was to examine, think, quest, discover, and to refine. One side argued that charismatic government gave authority through individuals to discern those who were being called to leadership and to recognize their call with ordination and placement. The other side held that God's call implies a call to preparation and that ordination naturally follows this process without being the exclusive right of any "bishop." One side held that education inevitably leads toward worldliness. Spirituality would be replaced by sophistry, and reformation principles would accommodate to the evils of Babylon. The other side argued that education opens up a broad, cultural stream and makes the treasure of the arts, letters, and science available to the young.

I am sure that F. G. Smith recognized early that the birth of the infant Bible School would inevitably threaten to destroy several of the central supports upon which his theological and ecclesiastical views were established. The infusion of education into the life of the church had been delayed now for thirty-six years. It was no longer to be denied. Still, the road was not to be an easy one.

The school did open that fall of 1917 in the Trumpet workers' home. This building had been originally constructed for the Trumpet Family in 1905-1906, in preparation for the move from Moundsville. Recently it had fallen into relative disuse when the company began to pay wages and families elected to move out into their own quarters. Scores of shanty houses sprang up in the area now occupied by the Warner Auditorium. The first students were young workers at the company, attending classes at night, under the tutelage of such persons as Russell and Bessie Byrum, John Phelps, Henry Clausen, and H. A. Sherwood. Although run on a shoestring, the school was regarded as a diversionary burden by principal officers of the company and barely made it into the second year.

Partly through the influence of my father, E. A. Reardon, who had been elected as the first chairman of the General Ministerial Assembly, permission had been granted for the Bible Training School. One fearful brother, however, rose to his feet and held forth mightily against the granting of diplomas as evidence of worldly conformity. The Assembly agreed, and the prohibition was mandated.

It was a tall, raw-boned, commanding figure named J. T. Wilson, then manager of Gospel Trumpet Company who, along with R. R. Byrum, managing editor, had laid plans for the school. It was to these far-sighted men, educational visionaries in their time, whom all of us owe more than we will ever know. Wilson, formerly an educator in Pennsylvania, had a genius for initiating programs far outweighing his management capabilities. Although he held the first administrative position as principal, he did not regard the office as a particularly important segment in his portfolio of responsibilities. While managing the Trumpet Company he also was responsible for erecting the Park Place church building at Eighth and Union Avenue, and organizing the Board of Church Extension and Home Missions. Wilson was an excessive spender, launching extensive and nearly ruinous financial schemes endangering the company and its workers. As a result, morale in the publishing plant fell to an all-time low.

A Coming Struggle

Let me now set the stage for the struggle which began in the early twenties and erupted a decade later. Brother Smith was not entirely secure in his editorial chair. More and more pastors were smarting under his authoritarian ways. Names were being withdrawn from the Yearbook. New leaders were emerging, calling for more democratic ways.

Early in 1919, Dr. Smith and my father had made a trip around the world to survey our missionary enterprise. During the trip Smith presented himself as the dominant and leading figure in the reformation. Although they were good friends, my father's Irish nature was severely tried by Smith's aggressive ways. By the time the trip was over, he had concluded that Smith was leading the reformation into the kind of sectarian wall-building that denied the very spirit of unity we were brought into being to foster. Father's diary had many references to long, earnest, but futile conversations with Smith on these matters. By 1920, my father was committed to a

In 1919 F. G. Smith (left) and E. A. Reardon made a world mission survey tour. Across the years the two leaders found much to oppose and to appreciate in each other.

change in editors, and the universal respect in which he was held helped to set the stage for what was about to transpire.

One must ponder carefully where F. G. Smith was coming from into the midst of these uneasy days. From all the original sources available, I think it not inaccurate to assume that he saw some troublesome handwriting on the wall. He felt the foundations of the movement were at stake, no less. As I have mentioned previously, the democratic spirit was gathering strength. It was being suggested that the editor had laid claim to too much authority and that God did work through the main body of the brethren to make his will known. Smith felt his strong opposition to organization and his theory of charismatic leadership being thereby challenged.

The ideal of unity in doctrine, the emergence again of the Truth freed from centuries of confusion and now articulated clearly and scripturally in standard Church of God literature, much of which he had written, was at stake. To give away this precious legacy, admitting to the possibility of other divergent views and interpretations held by sanctified believers, seemed to Smith to open the door to endless confusion. How could sanctified writers, led into all Truth by the Holy Spirit, be in error?

As Smith looked around he was aware that his fundational work, *Revelation Explained,* upon which he built the whole rationale for the last reformation, was being discretely undermined by a new brand of scholars whose views on prophetic literature did not match his own.

A central factor in this struggle was the growing influence of R. R. Byrum. Byrum, a nephew of Enoch, had come from Moundsville to help his father, Robert, a contractor, construct the Trumpet Home. Russell had come into the position as managing editor because of his hard work, bright mind, and scholarly writing as a Bible student and theologian. It was not long before he was dividing his energies between his editorial work and his classes at the school. Byrum read widely and was impressed by the views of A. T. Robertson and some of the other conservative scholars of the day. Byrum knew well what the so-called "standard" literature was. Byrum used Smith's books in class but also exposed students to other views.

This was a threat hard for Smith to bear. He could sit in his editor's chair and watch the students coming out of Byrum's classes across the street, excited by new ideas and full of questions about the old ways of thinking. He also was aware of the high regard in which his managing editor was held by members of his own staff.

A Strategy Emerges

Editor Smith was in trouble, and he began to work slowly and methodically to do what he thought was best to preserve and protect the church. His strategy was essentially the following.

1. *Remove J. T. Wilson as general manager.* Wilson, taking over more initiative and setting more programs in motion

than he could handle, appeared to be intruding on the prerogatives of the editor in chief. Smith wanted to replace him with someone on whom he could count for support. With worker morale running low and with severe financial problems that had come from Wilson's inclination to overextend company resources, the general

Left: R. R. and Bessie Byrum. Below, left: J. T. Wilson. Below, right: J. A. Morrison.

manager found himself out in 1923. D. W. Patterson, much at the instigation of R. R. Byrum and F. G. Smith, was brought in to replace him. Brother Wilson left Anderson a frustrated, beaten, and heartsick man. Shortly, he organized Warner Memorial University in Eastland, Texas, a venture which survived only a few years.

Not long before he left Anderson he had brought into the school, at the suggestion of R. R. Byrum, John A. Morrison, a promising young pastor from Delta, Colorado. This was the man who was destined to play a central role in the dramatic struggles of the next decade, struggles leading to the most crucial turning point in our history.

2. *Standardize the doctrine.* Smith sought to hold the line against losing the doctrinal clarity and forthrightness that had emerged with his writing. He urged in the General Ministerial Assembly that 1924 be established as a time line limiting the standard literature of the movement to the works published prior to that date. Fortunately that move failed.

3. *Replace R. R. Byrum as managing editor* and bring in a trusted lieutenant who could manage and exercise control over the editorial staff. In 1927 Byrum packed his bags and moved into a tiny office in Old Main. He made the move quickly for three reasons: First, he was drawn greatly to teaching and scholarly writing. Second, J. A. Morrison wanted and needed him badly and urged the move vigorously. Third, he was beginning to be a threat to F. G. whose editorial staff adored and greatly respected Byrum. Smith saw his chance to replace Byrum with R. L. Berry, who was amenable to Smith's views and directives. It was R. L. Berry, at Smith's urging, who brought about one of the worst, most useless, painful—and shameful—episodes in our history. We shall explore this event shortly.

4. *Contain, reduce, or eliminate the college.* Editor Smith, as we have seen, had always feared the influence of this

institution. He would seek to keep its influence at a minimum in every way possible. His opposition to R. R. Byrum was a part of this. His participation in efforts to oppose the college as a pastor after he left the editorial post was a continuation of his feelings.

By 1925, however, the school was coming on strong. Charter was granted, the prohibition against degrees was lifted, and one of the legendary figures in the movement, George Russell Olt, dean at Wilmington College in Ohio, was asked to join the faculty. His assignment: to build an accredited college and seminary for the church. Dean Olt was a man of extraordinary gifts. In some of his personal papers he mentions his own deepest interests. They were to (1) serve the church faithfully, (2) work for peace, (3) support racial equality, and (4) improve the lot of the laboring man through the labor movement.

Through years of hardship and suffering he doggedly worked away at broadening our educational horizons and laying plans for academic excellence. The Doctor of Philosophy degree was like the sound of celestial music to his ears, and he pushed incessantly to add credentialed people to the school. During the depression years he continued to minister to a Church of God congregation in Cincinnati, traveling there each week. His graduate work was at the University of Chicago, where he majored in psychology. It was his dogged determination to bring strength and integrity to the educational program that set the standard for a great deal of what has happened in higher education in the Church of God.

A Crucial Camp Meeting

The stage was set for camp meeting, 1929. The crash of the stock market underminded the nation's security badly. People were looking for stability and for scapegoats upon which to load their own frustrations and failures. By now, most of Byrum's students were rejoicing in the wine of new freedom. Many were exhilarated by exposure to new and interesting interpretations of the Scriptures. A few others fled to their pastors or to Brother Smith to relate how their fellow students were being led astray. Soon the word had spread to the far corners of the church. Now at camp meeting time things were at a boiling point. J. A. Morrison, who was chairman of the camp meeting committee, wrote E. A. Reardon, then pastoring the North Denver congregation, asking him to bring a message on the subject of unity in the June Assembly. He urged him to bring something both straightforward and thought-provoking. His urging was hardly needed. When the ministers gathered, he sent electric shocks through the brotherhood with some of the following statements:

There is no one place on earth from which God is directing all the affairs of his Kingdom, and his salvation work. There is no one body of people on earth who can claim an exclusive right to Christ and to all his light and truth. If Christ were here in person he would certainly put to confusion those bodies of his professed followers who make themselves his exclusive people. If Christ were here on earth today I cannot conceive of him as confining his operations exclusively to this movement.

Christ would certainly ignore our reformation exclusiveness and cultivate, first of all, that unity which is in himself. The expectation that all the sheep of the Lord in the world are eventually coming to us as a movement is not at all necessary to the success of God's plan.

I do suggest that we consider prayerfully why it is that we are so far away from others of God's people who have so large an amount of grace and truth, and why we have so little to do with them. Is it not a fact that while some of them have what we would say is 75 percent of the truth, yet we are not able to cooperate with them to the extent of 5 percent?

Many seem to have imbibed the spirit of exclusiveness to the extent that they are seriously prejudiced against even that which is good in others, simply because it does not have our stamp upon it. They have shut themselves up in the reformation and bolted the door.

One of our own brethren went to a revival held by a preacher who was not among us. He preached a good straight gospel and our good minister acknowledged that it was the truth but said he wasn't going in the back door of Babylon to get it. Such unreasonable and unchristlike statements are made of the worst kind of sectarian cloth.

As I look out upon the horizon of this movement, it seems to me that I can see a tendency to sectarianize it. If this tendency is allowed to go to seed it won't be long until we shall be numbered among the dead. I believe in a clean, separate, and distinct work for God, but I also believe that we should keep the sectarian stink out of the distinction. . . . There is such a thing as stressing the reformation to such an extent as to cause our people to be reformation centered—reformation sectarians.

We have among us, even yet, in some places a fair sprinkling of radicals who are so sectish in their view of this work, and so narrow in their vision, that God can never use them to hold aloft the lamp of truth. These good people may be striving earnestly for heaven, and we sometimes wish they were already there, for they certainly shut the door against many an honest soul and tie the hands of many a good pastor.

For a number of years now the soul of this movement has been striving to rid itself of this incubus so that its message might be carried as on eagle's wings. There are still among us those who would embalm the reformation and bury it in the iron casket of narrowness and extremism. They would make the reformation a fetish to be worshiped and not a vehicle of truth.

It would be a lonesome old world for us if we had to believe that all the work there is to be done in the world in carrying out God's plan had to be done by us.

If we get a clearer vision of His great work and a larger portion of the Spirit's power, this work will grow and nothing can stop it. On the other hand, if we yield to any influence that will sectarianize it we will soon fossilize and be in the Babylonian Museum ourselves.

—E. A. Reardon

After the shock waves were over, the ministers gathered in small groups all across the campground gesticulating, expounding, warning, and defending. Needless to say Brother Smith, R. L. Berry, C. E. Byers, and other conservative leaders were angry. The speaker had reached in and flayed the raw nerve of dissension that hitherto had been undisturbed. For the first time, the battle lines had been drawn in strong relief there before the whole Assembly. In the elections that year, father lost nearly every post. When the results were made public he rose before the Assembly. The air was electric with tension. What would he say? "I have seen the election results and I have only one thing to say, 'The brethren gave and the brethren have taken away. Blessed be the name of the brethren!" Nonetheless, the fat was in the fire.

The Russell Byrum "Trial"

Down at Park Place church basement the principal 1929 camp meeting struggle was going on. R. L. Berry, a college trustee and Dr. Smith's managing editor, had come to the board with a charge that R. R. Byrum was guilty of heresy in his teaching responsibilities. The bill of particulars set forth the claim that Byrum stressed a sociological approach rather than the guidance of the Holy Spirit into doctrinal unity, that sanctification was not given a central role in bringing about unity, that the supernatural in kingdom theology was not stressed, that his teaching undermined the faith of students in the

57

reformation movement and was the cause of much confusion. To meet this challenge the Board requested a panel of fifteen leading "thinking" ministers, with three trustees, to hear the case.

They were as follows: W. T. Wallace, C. E. Brown, E. E. Shaw, W. C. Gray, W. S. Sutherland, B. E. Warren, A. W. Miller, S. C. Smith, J. W. Lykins, W. J. Byers, Mabel Hale, E. G. Masters, H. M. Riggle, C. W. Naylor, D. W. Patterson; Trustees J. T. Wilson, S. P. Dunn, A. T. Rowe. R. L. Berry acted as the prosecutor, bringing the following to testify against Byrum: Swecker, Dale Oldham, I. S. McCoy, Otto Bolds, Paul Cook, Clifton Lord, F. G. Smith, E. E. Perry, R. C. Caudill, P. B. Turner, W. A. Parker, G. N. Neal, E. A. Fleenor, E. E. Byrum, and C. E. Bright. It was thought by the opposers that these persons had taken a position against Brother Byrum. J. A. Morrison pled the defense, J. T. Wilson sitting as the judge or chairman, and Dean Olt serving as secretary. Also, a parade of witnesses was asked to appear in Brother Byrum's behalf. They were Walter Haldeman, E. F. Adcock, N. H. Byrum, A. L. Byers, W. F. Coy, Burgess McCreary, John Kane, Herman Ast, F. W. Hopkins, and E. A. Reardon.

In a conversation much later with R. R. Byrum I learned that for some reason he was not notified of the trial but came anyway. The major point of controversy seemed to be over whether a person was really saved if he did not know the exact time it happened. The evangelists hammered away again and again, insisting that anyone who is saved must, by definition, know the time and place. Byrum carefully explained that there were some devout saints, active in the church today, who had labored in prayer for many hours and weeks before the peace of God finally fell upon their hearts—and, indeed, they could not recall the exact moment. On and on it went, day after weary day, some complaining that they wanted to be at services and not wasting their time on this.

Dale Oldham was originally one of the prosecution witnesses. But after he heard Byrum's explanation, he wrote a letter that very day explaining that he now understood and had changed his mind. Byrum never mentioned the letter which could have had a major effect on the proceedings.

During the trial one of the opposers, hardly one of our theological heavyweights, made a call at night on Byrum to get him straightened out. He announced that the Almighty had sent him with the word of truth. Byrum, not one to accept such counsel, fixed a cold eye on his visitor and remarked that if the Almighty was going to send him instructions it would be done by some one better informed.

After a sweltering, tension-filled week, the jury came to a conclusion. It voted with fair consistency on the charges—usually, eleven for exoneration, two to six against, and one or two neutral. The record, still in Wilson's penciled hand and affixed to the College Board minutes, reports the vote exonerating Byrum. It suggests that there was misunderstanding and points out that Byrum is a teacher, not an evangelist. It urges care in the future with doctrinal matters.

That night in the tower of the Gospel Trumpet building, R. R. Byrum submitted his resignation. The minutes report that the opposition was not satisfied and that the resignation was not acted on. We may never know the pain and agony wrapped in such a scene. The opposers lost, but they represented a roster of some of the most powerful men in the church. They went home angry and frustrated, vowing that another day would come. What a week! In a few short days Reardon's sermon had stunned them like a bomb, Byrum had been exonerated, and they had lost the day. Now the conflicts had come to the surface. They stayed on the agenda in the church, festering for the next four years.

In the Wake of the Trial

How was the Byrum affair resolved? There are misunderstandings here that we will perhaps never fathom. Brother Byrum was obviously deeply hurt. Byrum later explained that no one told him how the vote came out and that he left the college because he thought the administration really wanted him to and now regarded him as a political liability. I received the strong impression that he felt betrayed by those who should have urged him to continue. Dr. Morrison's report is somewhat different. He felt that Brother Byrum's resignation was worded in such a way that he could not be persuaded to stay on. So, in our well-meaning folly, each side contending for what it felt to be the right, we lost one of the fine minds in the service of the church. It should be some consolation to Brother Byrum, however, that his systematic theology has stood the test of time perhaps better than any other of our publications written at that time.

After the exit of R. R. Byrum from the school in spite of overwhelming exoneration, there was a growing restlessness among some of the progressive brethren who looked for a change in the editor's office. It was their judgment that the skill and great influence of F. G. Smith was dominating the affairs of the movement in a heavy-handed way. Morrison knew that Smith would continue to use the full weight of his office to contain the school. For years Reardon had been convinced that Smith should go. A.T. Rowe, influential pastor who would soon become general manager of the Trumpet Company, could be counted on to agree. Since Smith needed to be ratified in 1930, they began to make their plans to bring in a new editor.

The Editor Replaced

So at camp meeting time, 1930, over in the Trumpet Company office, the Publication Board members assembled to elect the editor for another term. Things were not going well. Largely at the instigation of Morrison, Rowe, and Reardon, thirteen of the twenty-four members of the company had vowed that they had had enough and that they would not give Brother Smith the majority needed for his reelection. They held fast in spite of much churning, and as an alternative brought forth and elected H. M. Riggle, the Billy Graham of the movement. The next day the Assembly, angered by Smith's rejection, voted Riggle down. So the company members reassembled and went at it again. The thirteen held fast, and there was nothing to do but find an alternate. C. E. Brown was nominated and finally agreed to serve if F. G. Smith himself would go to the General Ministerial Assembly and endorse him. To Brother Smith's great credit he did just that (as did Brother Riggle), but the defeated editor carried in his heart the bleeding sore of loss. This all had been a stunning blow to the conservatives.

Brother Smith's great devotion to the church was evident in his magnanimous gesture to endorse C. E. Brown as the new editor in chief. Yet, even while moving on to evangelistic work and the pastorate of a key congregation in Akron, Ohio, he carried with him a sad and bleeding heart. Rejection is a heavy blow, especially for those who feel a sense of mission and calling in what they do. But time would pass, and in the days ahead he would regain strength. A majority of his neighboring pastors in Ohio would rally again to his support.

Nevertheless, the church had come through a turning point. In its effort to walk in the light, it had started to move beyond the leadership of a few gifted individuals into a more democratic process where it was assumed God would speak to and through the larger body in leading his people.

Chapter 4
Learning and the Light

The young college in Anderson remained a prime target of the "last reformation" forces in the church following the change of editors in 1930. It had been a major part of F. G. Smith's plan while editor either to eliminate or contain the school. There can be no doubt that both E. E. Byrum and Smith saw the college, particularly in the form of a liberal arts institution, as a serious threat. They did not feel that such a school drawing on knowledge of the past ought to be a top priority for a reformation movement which was out to spread its message around the world. Indeed, a college which dealt in the marketplace of ideas was to be watched and closely monitored.

Smith, E. E. Byrum, and others were agreed that John A. Morrison, the college's president, could not be trusted. Morrison was a principal player in the drama now unfolding. Of disarming charm and wit, with uncanny insights into human personality, political savvy, and determined loyalty for the college—he had no equals. In an age of heavy sermonizing, he could be counted on always for a few good laughs. He was a persuader of unexcelled ability.

A Toothache Felt Across the Country

After Morrison took over as principal, one of his first acts was to bring Russell Olt, dean of Wilmington College, to campus. I have mentioned before Olt's degree in psychology. Given the tensions of the early thirties,

Russell Olt became first dean of Anderson College.

one event that took place didn't do much to calm Morrison's nerves. Dean Olt's secretary, Mary Husted, had an abscessed tooth which needed to be pulled. Olt went down to Dr. Rollie Bennett, a new dentist in town, and asked if he would be willing to try a revolutionary experiment. Would he pull the tooth under hypnosis? "Be glad to," said Bennett. It all went beautifully. Dean Olt hypnotized Mary, the tooth came out, and the pair were jubliant.

Straightway they went to the office of the *Anderson Herald* and gave a full account of what had transpired. Alas, the story hit the Associated Press wires and went buzzing from coast to coast. Lowell Thomas included it in his nightly radio broadcast. When the brethren heard the news, storm signals went up all across the land. Letters denouncing devil worship and wizzardry began to pour in, and in spite of an open meeting in the old chapel in which the dean sought to allay fears, the angry clouds began to gather again over the college.

To Live or Die for the Last Reformation

It was 1933, and it had now been three years since Brother Smith had left office to do evangelistic work and finally to accept the pastorate of the church in Akron, Ohio. As a pastor he was highly successful, and in leadership among the Ohio church constituents he had no peer. I have tried here to put on paper what might be a fair statement of the feeling of many of the Ohio brethren and why there was so much hostility directed against Morrison and the school. The last reformation, its message, claims, experiences—this was their life. They were certain that this message of truth was divinely sanctioned, validated in scriptural prophecy, and was live and pulsating in their midst. They saw their mission to teach it, proclaim it, defend it, sacrifice for it, and if necessary die for it. They held that the reformation was a sacred trust and that it must not be permitted to be drawn away from its ordained path in any way. Therefore, the college must be silenced as a mortal enemy standing in the way of divine fulfillment of the last reformation dream. In addition, a practical problem loomed on the horizon. Without doubt, the college would soon send out pastors with educational credentials in place of Holy Ghost ordination. Pastors could see themselves crowded out by John Morrison's boys. This was taken as a serious threat and greatly aggravated the situation.

The Springfield Resolution

The first indication of action came in a resolution condemning the college which was by the ministers gathered at Springfield in August, 1933. In the official minutes of the College Board of Trustees, the copy of the resolution is accompanied by a letter from Dale Oldham, secretary, Ohio State Ministerial Association, under the date of September 2, 1933:

Dear Brother Morrison:

Great grace and peace be unto you, for you surely need a double portion. It is with much regret that I send you the enclosed Resolution, passed the other day at Springfield while I was absent at Warner Camp.

I shall earnestly pray that God will have His way in this matter. Of course I realize that if the suggested path is taken in the matter that it means the loss to the movement of all such great teachers as Olt, Kardatzke, and others.

May God give you the fortitude of Paul, the wisdom of Solomon, the hide of a rhinoceros, and more brotherly love than any one man should ever be expected to need, as you face the future.

Yours in Christ,

W. Dale Oldham, Secretary
OHIO STATE MINISTERIAL ASSOCIATION

The main points of the Springfield Resolution were as follows:

1. It called attention to textbooks which introduced theories that contradicted standard Bible doctrine.
2. Non-theological courses were causing much friction in the ministry.
3. There was no other school devoted to the propagation of the full gospel as now revealed to the "Church of God."
4. It was useless to compete with the public colleges and universities.
5. The college should be reorganized into a Bible school with a curriculum restricted to the teaching of standard literature of the Church of God.
6. The Board of Trustees was asked to frame a resolution to accomplish these things before the General Assembly in June, 1934.

Having received a number of resolutions myself, I know the kind of feeling it engendered in John Morrison and his staff. It was not a complaint from a few disgruntled preachers. It was a life-and-death ultimatum. Responding to a challenge from the largest center of influence in the movement was going to be a battle down to the wire, calling for every resource at the disposal of the college. The Springfield Resolution was followed by a second resolution, framed in Toledo at the meeting of the Ohio Assembly on December 28, 1933.

There were several strategic reasons for the timing of the effort to close the school. It had been three years now since Dr. Smith's bitter defeat and the hostility engendered by the R. R. Byrum trial. It was a time for organizing and consolidating the opposition. Also, time was of the essence. Each year that went by more and more alumni were moving out into places of leadership on the field, and *The Gospel Trumpet* was beginning to come on with more moderate, scholarly views under Dr. Brown's leadership. Finally, and most important, it was the year in which Morrison would need to have his election to another term ratified by the General Ministerial Assembly. This ratification served as a major, visible, and open target. A bare majority was needed to bring Morrison down and the Ohio brethren were sure they could rally the votes. So four days after Christmas, 1933, the stage was set in Toledo where the ministers of Ohio met to pass a second resolution to accomplish just that.

The Toledo Resolution

The Toledo Resolution was a declaration of war. Gathered in Toledo, the Ohio pastors were worked into a militant state by C. E. Byers, state chairman and pastor of the large Maiden Lane Church of God in Springfield, as well as by F. G. Smith and others. Emotional speeches charged the air with electricity, and at the right moment a prepared resolution was brought forth. It is too long to include here, but it began by "whereasing" that there have been grave questions existing all across the nation about doctrinal teaching at Anderson College undermining the reformation. It went on to resolve that Ohio would neither give more dollars nor would it send more students to the college; by implication it would place no more graduates in state pastorates until the college was closed, the administration replaced, and a Bible school restored. This school would be completely committed to standard reformation truth and would carry a "burning reformation emphasis."

The resolution was sent out to all ordained ministers in the *Yearbook*, with an explanatory note signed by C. E. Byers. The note informed the readers that the resolution had the endorsement of the entire state ministry and was not a call for independence, but a stand representative of where the vast majority of saints and pastors in all states stood. Here, wrote Byers, was a statement of principle and a call for action. Needless to say, the resolution became a rallying point for the like-minded all across the church.

To Defend and Justify the Attack

That spring, on April 2 and 3, the ministers met again in Columbus, Ohio, for a council of war. They soon realized that there were some new fronts to consider and some defenses of their own to make. Some were asking: Why were they making trouble? Were they going to split the body? Why were they so opposed to education? Why crucify the brethren who had established the school?

After the meeting Brother Byers wrote again to the *Yearbook* list a three-and-a-half page, single-spaced letter which he used to defend and justify the attack. The letter makes the following points:

1. As chairman of the Ohio Association, following distribution of the Toledo Resolution, I have been buried

under an avalanche of mail from all across the country, expressing the strongest agreement. This letter serves to reply since I could not possibly reply personally.

2. We are not agitators. We ministers have kept these matters in closest confidence among ourselves until the college went public with the problem.

3. The college was "put over on us" in 1928, without due consideration, and needs reconsideration. This was not an irrevocable decision by the General Ministerial Assembly.

4. We are waiting for the college to declare their commitment to teach the Truth as published in our standard literature. We *know* that a different brand of unity is being taught.

5. Secular truth, the concern of colleges, is subject to various interpretations. But Bible unity, based on Truth divinely and authoritatively revealed in our standard literature, is the only center to which all Christians can be brought. The two cannot be mixed.

6. Colleges are built by denominations. We are not a denomination.

7. In Ohio we are in a period of glorious harmony. It is institutionalism that is breeding discord.

8. Catholics and Lutherans have become slaves to the colleges they started. Their pulpits do not control their colleges. The colleges control the pulpits.

9. God's true Church must stand on Bible Truth only, free from secular and worldly entanglements.

10. And finally, if the ministers do not vote to close the college, we do insist that Morrison go and that he be replaced with someone completely doctrinally sound and grounded in the reformation Truth.

I am intrigued by a letter of response in our archives from Otto Linn, written to F. G. Smith, Rachel Lord, and C. E. Byers, supposed drafters of the resolution. (Linn added the D.D. conferred on F. G. Smith by the college, in the salutation.) The letter, written in the scholarly manner for which this distinguished educator was

C. E. Byers, pastor at Springfield, Ohio, led a 1933 attack on College policies.

Otto F. Linn, Bible teacher and author, was a figure in the 1933 controversy.

known, asked why he had not been visited by the Ohio brethren since, indeed, it was in his field that so much of the accusation of heretical teaching lay. He stated that his teachings had never been questioned. What were these charges?

I have in hand the letter of reply to Dr. Linn from F. G. Smith. It is a masterpiece. He indicated that the college had not been responsive in the past to messages from the field, and that the Toledo Resolution was drafted and circulated so that these grievances could not be ignored any longer. Smith pointed out that the matter had been an open sore during the past five or six years, from coast to coast, and that the fault lay in the management of the school, not necessarily with all those connected with it. Smith then pointed out that Linn would not be injured in the coming shake-up if he maintained his loyalty to "the Cause we all love so well."

Smith closed his letter with this interesting caution and subtle suggestion:

> I may be going too far in even suggesting what you should do; but there is a reason for it. I *know* that the eyes of some well-known ministers, not only in Ohio but outside of Ohio, are upon you. The suggestion has been made (and from outside of Ohio) that *you* should be the head of that institution. It seems certain that changes there must be; for no church institution can succeed without general confidence and support, any more than can a local pastor succeed (notwithstanding many partisan supporters) so long as a large section of his congregation have lost confidence in his leadership and insist on maintaining a non-cooperative attitude.

Fortunately, Dr. Linn was not in the least moved by these suggestions.

The College Replies

During the months that followed, little else was on the minds of our pastors and church leaders. Although it must be assumed that F. G. Smith was a principal strategist for the Ohio brethren, it was C. E. Byers who was out front. Byers, as the pastor of Maiden Lane church, was a real power in Springfield. He was law and gospel in central Ohio, bringing on men in the ministry, seeing that they were ordained and placed. The campground at Springfield was controlled largely by the Maiden Lane congregation and was the staging ground for opposition against the school.

During the spring of 1934 the battle raged, with the opposers crying, "Close the college!" "Remove the president!" In Old Main lights burned late at night in the offices of Morrison and Olt, who were trying to counteract the onrushing tide. Morrison's reply to the two resolutions came out in the spring issue of the *Broadcaster*, official college publication sent to all ministers and alumni.

His message was skillfully drafted, conceding the good and pure motives of his opposers, allowing that various views were appropriate. In his reply he affirmed his devotion to the Church of God and its central truths. He spoke modestly about his own qualifications for office. He pointed to the more than five hundred young men and women who had gone out to serve the church and their deep sense of dedication. He then laid the groundwork to defend the college. What about the twenty-five thousand young people among us who wanted a Christian education? His plea went on to point out the financial support needed from tuition to make the whole operation go. He then pointed out what a calamity it would be to close the college and embarrass graduates who held diplomas from the college. He noted the increase in enrollment and the largest freshman class in history, and called upon the church to rally to preserve one of its greatest assets.

A second message raised the ugly specter—the disgrace of a split in the church—and chided the Ohio brethren for not calling in college teachers and leaders to counsel with them before firing their guns.

During this tense time, my father was Morrison's closest friend and adviser. They often walked out the old interurban tracks to Jackson's Crossing (now the bridge by the airport). It was a gloomy time. Students were leaving for lack of funds. The great depression had a stranglehold on the nation. The faculty were paid in scrip because money was nowhere to be had, and the ominous rumblings of warfare were echoing in Ohio. On a particularly cold January night, the two were walking silently, deep in their own thoughts, returning to the campus along the tracks. It was about six o'clock in the evening and the lights were just beginning to flicker on in

Old Main as they stopped by the old tabernacle (now Byrum Hall). Sensing Morrison's mood of despair, my father laid his hand on the beleaguered president's shoulder, lifted a hand toward Old Main, and said, "See those lights coming on, J. A? We're never going to let them go out!" Later, Morrison, in recalling the struggles of those days, would put his hands behind his head, lean back in his office chair, and with misty eyes say, "That was a moment I'll never forget."

President Morrison was a fighter. He could sense a battle coming, sniff out the strategy of the opposition, and lay his own plan of defense. He had plenty of practice. He used to say to me, "Never get in a fight unless you are sure you are right and sure you can win." Alas, things would have gone better for me had I listened to his advice. He also had a practice that he followed when things were rough. He walked in the cemetery till he got himself under control. Space will not permit the inclusion of any of the avalanche of mail that arrived, in the wake of these two resolutions. Some of it was abusive, calling for his resignation. Some was encouraging. But Morrison knew he was in the battle of his life for the school and planned his own strategy.

His approach went something like this. Get things solid at home. This he did through faculty and trustee meetings, hour after hour, to insure that the base was solid. Next he began to get the alumni organized and ready for action. A call went out all across the country to alumni to attend a homecoming at campmeeting time. The *Broadcaster* went to three-and four-page layouts, printing the resolutions and Morrison's replies. The message was the same: "Save the College! Don't let the unity of the movement be broken!"

E. A. Reardon and A. T. Rowe agreed to get out to ministers meetings all across the country to counteract the hostility being engendered. "Morrison is the George Washington of the college," A. T. Rowe said. Finally, Morrison made it clear that his own position was not important but that the school must go on with or without him. The writing in the *Broadcaster* was masterfully done. It did not attribute low motives, ignorance, or lack of ethics to the Ohio brethren. It did put the issues on the line in a skillful manner, perhaps not enough to change minds, but by generosity and good grace to neutralize some.

Some Days in June

In June the crowds began to pour in. There was no other agenda on anyone else's mind than the settling of this struggle. Embroiled in it were all the strongest and most influential personalities of the movement. The following is a chronological account of the events which followed:

Thursday, June 14: Trustees met. Morrison offered to resign. Not accepted.

Saturday, June 16: C. E. Byers called for a meeting of opposing ministers with the college Board of Trustees to demand action. He threatened to take the matter to the Assembly if the Board refused. Board refused.

Monday, June 18: The ballot was distributed in the Assembly. The time had come to decide. Some 474 ministers took pen in hand and voted their convictions on whether or not President Morrison should be removed.

Tuesday, June 19: The tellers posted the ballot out on the bulletin board near the lunch stand, and a crowd immediately appeared. *For* Morrison—243: *against*—231. The vote was essentially to decide whether or not to continue the college and to continue its present leadership. The decision was by a twelve-vote margin. But it was a decision far more profound than that. At stake was how the church was to address itself in the future—as a cult, calcified, turned in, windows closed; or as a people twice liberated from the rule of new and sterile creeds. I believe that no other single action by the Assembly has had more effect on the future of the Church of God movement. And we can be grateful for the men and women whose vision of the church was so true that they suffered, fought, and persevered for the principles that we enjoy today.

Tuesday, June 19, p.m.: C. E. Byers asked the Board of Trustees to consider a plan to divorce the college from the Assembly and build a reformation Bible school in Winchester, Kentucky, under the supervision of the GMA. The Board agreed to appoint a committee at once to discuss the plan. Byers, F. G. Smith, P. B. Turner, R. C. Caudill, and J. W. Reuhle met with A. F. Gray, W. C. Gray, W. E. Monk, Elver Adcock, and Dean Olt to discuss the plan.

Wednesday, June 20, evening: By this time, Dean Olt had had enough and was weary of the long struggle with the Ohio brethren. In the meeting which followed he leaned toward the proposed plan with the following provisions:

1. The college curriculum would remain unchanged.

2. The Kentucky Bible school would remain strictly a Bible school with standard Bible school curriculum.

3. If the college withdrew from the control of the Assembly, all fighting would stop.

4. The college would remain recognized as a church-related college, with promotion in *The Gospel Trumpet* and other publications of the movement.

Essentially, the Wednesday night meeting of the principals on both sides was an effort at reconciliation. Each side was exhausted from the strain of battle, and neither had much enthusiasm for plan-making. Fortunately, the ideas of separation did not prevail. Prayer, suffering, hostility, reaching toward each other, backing away—all were endured; but when the Assembly met the next day a statement of unreserved commitment to the movement and to one another was read.

In their mature years, F. G. Smith and J. A. Morrison met, broke bread together, and came to a blending of spirits drawn from the deepest wells of human existence—a common Lord, a common faith, and a profound love and commitment for the church. Together they found validating evidence of the centrality of that unity of the spirit which transcends the doctrinal impulse to seek unity in creed and ritual. F. G. and J. A. have now entered into that celestial city where our human frailties and the struggle to comprehend the Truth are only shadows of yesterday. There the lamp of Truth shines forth in its majestic brightness and eternal flame.

The old Gospel Trumpet workers' home at Anderson served for many years as the main building at Anderson College.

Chapter 5
Looking at the Early Light

Perhaps we are now far enough removed from the first fifty years of our movement to look back with some perspective. We are urged by historians to study the past, seek out our mistakes, and learn from them lest we repeat the same mistakes again. This view of history is urged upon us more by the old-fashioned wisdom which counsels: "Any dogcatcher that gets bit twice by the same dog deserves to be a dogcatcher." In viewing the past it is well also to get a clear view of the conflicts going on in order to understand the source of the many problems, crises, and confrontations which existed during this first half-century of our work. Time will permit me only to touch on them briefly.

Crises and Conflicts

1. *The conflict between the individual charismatic leadership principle and the democratic charismatic leadership theory*: Looking at the first fifty years of our movement, one should never underestimate the depth of populist sentiment in the Midwest, the rugged individualism, and the near religious attachment there was to the ballot box. The right to *voice* and *vote* could hardly be walled out of the movement and began to make its appearance with the earliest assemblies. In these assemblies ministers began to vote. Some were voted in; others were voted out. Decisions were made by vote of the community. Sound the alarm! So came the word from Anderson. Since when were those appointed and ordained in

leadership roles to be subject to the evils of organization and the precedents established by the denominations? By and large the movement, in its first fifty years, was directed by an autocratic group of strong leaders, the chief being the editor of the *Trumpet*. Others came to power principally through sheer strength of leadership ability and preaching power. At its best, the view that God directs the church through the endowment of spiritual authority in individuals gave rise to a process of natural selection which brought to the fore men and women of great strength and enabled them to move without the encumbrances of the slow, tedious, democratic process. In local churches, pastors might claim to be called to leadership and be accepted by congregations with few formalities, but they rarely stayed unless they could really deliver the goods. They established their place partly through their ability to dominate the congregation by expounding the truth, laying down the law on conduct, disciplining the nonconforming, appointing members to various tasks, and silencing rivals. Some strong congregations were built around these leaders and their influence was pervasive throughout the church.

At its worst, some little tyrants bulldozed their way with the standard command: *"This* is *your* place. The Lord has revealed to me that you should do this." But with the democratic impulse so strong in the land, this domination of the flock by individuals claiming divine authority to order others about was soon in trouble. Some of the first cracks in the dike were the establishment of the asemblies, and that mean little device despised by every pastor, the yearly vote of confidence by secret ballot. The handwriting of defeat was on the wall in the declining years of E. E. Byrum as editor. Perhaps the folly of our ways in these matters is best illustrated by the preacher who wrote to an attractive prospective mate with this final plea: "The Lord has definitely revealed to me, whilst on my knees all through the night in prayer, that you should marry me." After signing his name, he penned a quick postscript, "Please answer at once on account of I have several others in mind."

Wrapped up also in this conflict is the whole question of where authority is lodged. Is it in the individual or the group? If the first three editors were asked, their answers would most certainly have been that the Bible and the Holy Spirit in the heart of the believer is where authority rests. If you varied from standard doctrine and conduct, however, a note would appear in the *Trumpet* simply stating that Brother X is no longer in fellowship with this movement. If a churchly or doctrinal question arose, a search would be made in the "standard literature" and if no clear answer appeared, a question would be sent to the editor; the reply in the *Trumpet* became law and gospel. The struggle to keep a doctrinally sound community of belief while at the same time making room for individuals who dare think their own thoughts before the Lord—this has been the source of much tension.

2. *The conflict between eradication, perfectionism, and spiritual infilling.* I have no doubts about the utter dedication of Warner and others. It was total and without reservation. It came as a traumatic, complete renunciation of self, family, and carnal desires. One can only stand in profound awe. The consuming appetite after holiness in Warner's life is closely akin to Francis of Assisi, Augustine, and others. As Warner sought to understand this experience he found his theology primarily in the writings of the holiness movement.

Not content with Wesley, the nineteenth century holiness theologians were coming forward with more radical views. Principal among these was the eradication theory. This theory held that sanctification was a supernatural experience subsequent to conversion, which brought about a total eradication of one's natural instincts—defined as one's carnal nature—and burned out one's inclination to sin. Warner was quick to fasten on this experience as the key which opened the door to all truth. He saw sanctification as the method which restored primitive New Testament theology and life. He saw it as the means by which sanctified ones would perceive the evils of sectism, renounce Babylon, and "come out" into the pure light of God's restored Church. It was his foundation stone for unity. As time went on the emphasis tended to become harsh and mechanical. The ideal of perfection came to be measured by adherence to a well-defined code of conduct, and impossible claims were made.

A young mother, worn with the demands of small children, meals, housework, and the labors of washing clothes by hand in a tub, looks outside to find her freshly laundered clothing lying in the mud. The eradication preachers said that a sanctified heart would respond by singing praises to God. A woman who responded otherwise, in anger and frustration, either refused to face this anger honestly and drove her guilt feelings underground or she had to conclude that she had never been sanctified at all.

Working against this radical view was the problem of validating the eradication doctrine with human experience. Few women really felt like praising the Lord when the laundry fell in the mud. Few honest men could claim that there were not moments when some of their most carnal desires were very near the surface. Often, our most devout and sensitive saints were driven back to the altar in frustration and guilt to seek an experience they knew they did not have. This great quest in the reformation movement brought out some of the most saintly personalities I have ever known. Alas, the distortion of this beautiful doctrine, given for comfort, infilling, empowering, joy, and peace, became for some a burden to be borne. It developed some grotesque characters among us who became harsh, judgmental, suspicious, and altogether foreign to the sweet graces of Christian character. It was C. E. Brown who took us by the hand and helped us know that that which was

Editor Charles E. Brown was a moderating voice in eradication theology, church government, and historical interpretation.

sanctified was that which belonged to God, and that it was the presence and power of the Holy Spirit that brought wholeness and health into our lives to direct and control our humanness.

Eradication theology did not wear well with intelligent, honest, human experiences. It is a tragedy that problems such as I have described have come dangerously close to shelving a priceless doctrinal treasure in our emphasis these last fifty years.

3. *Conflict over the nature of Truth.* This conflict was a central struggle, almost always the final ground of our disagreements, during the first fifty years. Warner, Byrum, and Smith, our first three editors, saw Truth as a body of doctrinal light breaking forth upon the scene. It was to be distinguished from secular or scientific truth—this being the province of the secular world. The

"evening light Truth" had to do with a revelation and restoration of a body of Truth over which the primitive church had exercised jurisdiction before the great Apostasy. It was like a beautiful gift from God entrusted to the saints to be heralded abroad, written, and preached about. And it was to be defended at all costs. To be fair, I think our early leaders would hardly have argued that they knew *all* the Truth there was to know. More light was "sweetly dawning." The conflict, however, arose when Russell Byrum took his scholarly key and demanded entrance into our doctrinal museum to raise questions about some of the exhibits there. It has always been the impulse of organized religion to articulate a body of knowledge as endowed with a kind of divine sanction. The Talmudic writings, and papal encyclicals are examples. In our work, *What the Bible Teaches* and *Revelation Explained* were moving rapidly in this direction. Consequently, tampering with these teachings, examining them, raising questions about them, was resisted, feared, and made R. R. Byrum and others subject to the accusation of heresy. Was not "this Truth" associated with our deepest emotions, sung by our poets, published in our standard literature? Shame! Out with the traitors!

Yet, slowly and with irresistible force, young minds and old, honest before God and dedicated to the Truth that sets people free, continued to search and wrestle with the Scriptures, persistently refusing blind acquiescence to a dogmatic view of Truth. When Morrison was ratified by that slim margin of twelve votes, it was more than a simple ratification of a man. It was a vote of confidence for a whole new approach to Truth. From this time on our pastors, teachers, students have been free to think, explore, to be open before the Lord of all Truth, to rejoice and exult in what we have found of its majesty and beauty. We have been free to move on without fear toward undreamed of, unimagined coasts.

Off the Track

Let us turn now to take a candid look at some of the places where we got off the track, and why.

1. *Extremism.* The most dangerous people in any reform movement may be the extremists who advocate it. This extremism is generally characterized by pushing a valid thing to its outward boundaries where it becomes distorted and untenable. Take emotionalism, for example. Although Warner often warned against excesses of emotionalism, the inspired preaching at camp meeting really turned the people on. Shouting and jumping were common. One sincere brother, not given to such outbursts, was troubled about his experience since his feet stayed solidly on the ground. He was advised to go across the tracks into the cemetery and practice jumping in the area where this writer is fortunate now to reside. No doubt some jumped in while others jumped out.

Other extremes had to do with dress—rarely men's dress, although few can forget the battle that raged over the necktie problem. Women in those early days were supposed to look like shapeless peasants—plain, dull, and altogether unattractive. Generally, there was one sister in every congregation who felt called to carry on a constant surveillance lest any of the saints came forth in gold or any finery on the no-no list. For some unknown reason, she always was equipped with eyes like a hawk to seek out that extra tuck or bit of embroidery. It was her self-appointed assignment to make her way to the altar to advise women converts of their new freedom to divest themselves of every ornament and vestage of carnal vanity.

This abomination afflicted us for years and made life entirely miserable. It had a deadly cumulative effect—like hazing on a college campus. The victims, in their suffering and humiliation, say "Just wait till the next candidate comes along." And so each generation becomes more fanatical.

So also did extremism surface in our Babylon-thrashing sermons. Often they became abusive, ugly, and far from the gentle spirit of the Master. Dr. W. E. Reed tells of a conversation with F. G. Smith, in Smith's later years after he had returned to Anderson. "Why," he asked Brother Smith, "have you quit thrashing Babylon?" Smith replied, "Because as a pastor I found that my major energies were needed to build up the walls of Zion."

Probably no extremes went so far as those connected with divine healing. The contract method of healing left no room for injury or illness. Illness became an onus to bear as though something in your life had not been surrendered. Resort to a physician or medicine was evidence of a lack of faith and destroyed the contract. Many precious souls had to bear both their pain and the agony of guilt when they were not healed.

Those excesses, fortunately, are not very much with us today in the movement. However, one has only to turn on the TV to see our Lord portrayed as a kind of celestial witch doctor who comes running at the bidding of show-biz personalities to bring release from all pain in our distorted lives, satisfy our every childish whim, and remove every obstacle. All of this is meant to send us into flights of ever-intensifying spiritual ecstasy and make everything sweet and beautiful. Many are leading the credulous off into religious excesses, often through fantastic promises of what God is going to do: everything from fixing the plumbing, to shielding *your* farm alone from the ravages of the ice storm, revealing which girl to marry, which stock to buy, when to trade your old car in and, in case of need, where to get a shot of miracle gas in your empty tank. These merchandisers of God's grace, holding forth in television temples, will need to answer to God for what they do. They surely must do some good, but they often fall into that ancient trap of the enemy which was laid for the Master when he urged Jesus to jump from the pinnacle of the Temple—the

Thousands gathered each June in the old frame tabernacle at Anderson to hear the best-known preachers of the movement. The structure served for some forty years before being replaced by Warner Auditorium.

temptation to put on stunts and to please the crowd.

2. *Narcissism.* In ancient Greek mythology, Narcissus fell in love with his own reflection as he gazed into a pool of water. From the very beginning, Warner and others held a high view of the Church. It was the Church, restored after years of division and darkness; the Church, the Bride of Christ; the Church, the pillar and ground of the Truth; the Church, gathered in these last days. As time passed, much writing began to focus on who *we* are. This preoccupation often led us away from the Christ whose message of redemption we were called to deliver.

3. *Dogmatism.* It was clear from the writings of Warner, E. E. Byrum, Smith, and others that they regarded the reformation as a reemergence of doctrinal truth, coming forth first in the sixteenth century, but incomplete because of its captivity in the denominations. Now the decayed walls of sectish Babylon were crumbling and the light was bursting forth anew. The key to doctrinal purity was *sanctification.* The wholly sanctified scholar was led by the Holy Spirit into all Truth and, consequently, its discovery and proclamation would be free from error and disagreement. Often the reformation movement was called "The Truth" and it was thought to be delivered, full-orbed, to the saints as their doctrinal standard. Smith held that the unity sought in bringing together a united church would by definition need to be a church wholly joined together in doctrinal agreement.

The first crack in the view that "we have the Truth, the whole Truth, and nothing but the Truth" came in a strange way. It had to be faced in the necktie question. We saints had been wrong about something! Alas, today we have gone so far to the other extreme that many of our congregations have drifted into a vacuous, mindless, emotional religious rock band, exhibiting fun-time religion accurately described by Bonhoffer as "cheap grace." The search for Truth, the practice of it, and the testing of it provide a continuing challenge to the church. It is there. But our perception of it is never so complete that we can claim an exclusive franchise to it. At one time we came very close to doing just that and insisting that other Christians must lay aside their own views and espouse our standard literature as evidence of their obedience to renounce sectism and "come out into reformation light." At this point in our history we came dangerously close to taking our eyes off Christ, the way, the truth, and the life, and going down into the deep water with Peter.

4. *Exclusivism.* For most of our first fifty years we practiced a high degree of exclusiveness with the watchword, "Be ye not unequally yoked together with unbelievers." The unbelievers were thought to be those both in sin and Babylon. That left precious few besides ourselves. This exclusiveness manifested itself in complete separation from other religious groups. It meant complete separation from the local ministerial association, religious councils, and refusal to join in Good Friday or Easter Sunrise services. Ewald Wolfram paraphrases one of our songs as follows, "We reach our hands in fellowship to every foot-washed one." Pastors who "let down the standard" and broke over were scorned as selling out the reformation. The view that God had abandoned the denominations and was no longer at work in them left us with a very difficult position to defend: namely, that God was restricting his activity to our reformation movement. Fortunately, this impossible assumption did not prevail.

Our Mission and Destiny

I have labored in the preceding paragraphs to lift up some of the problem areas of the first fifty years. For the most part, the passage of time has helped us get beyond these encumbrances to our mission. It seems, however, apparent to this writer that our most serious problem has been to redefine our mission and identity. Consider the chief pillar in the house, a prophetic calculation that identified us in Scripture with a great reformation beginning in 1880, destined to restore the Church and herald the end of the age. We must admit that this view unleashed a powerful driving force. For those who "saw the light" it was an illuminating, confirming, exciting experience, something really to shout about.

When A. W. Miller, Otto Linn, and others began to examine the validity of arguments put forward in last reformation theology, the movement began to undergo an identity crisis of major proportions. An open, honest, scholarly look at the Book of Revelation simply would not support the previous conclusions expounded by F. G. Smith and others. Otto Linn, perhaps the most distinguished of our New Testament scholars, wrote in his trilogy of New Testament Studies published in 1941, that John the Revelator is careful to impress upon his readers that his prophecy is concerned with the immediate future, "things which must shortly come to pass" (Rev. 1:1). Does Babylon refer to the Protestant denominations? Linn said: impossible."The name Babylon refers unmistakable to Rome." The call to "come out of her," Linn insisted to mean that the early Christians were not to be corrupted with the moral degeneracy and the evils of the pagan world around them. It was C. W. Naylor who called on the church to "stop preaching theories of prophecy which few will ever believe," and it was the special vision of C. E. Brown which began to move our foundations to firmer historical ground.

This writer holds that the collapse of "last reformationism" which began to appear among us in the twenties and thirties left a central theological vacuum, an identity crisis, which cannot be underestimated in the traumatic effect it has had on the movement. Gone, it seemed to leave us lost on the scene without distinctives, without identity and without comrades in arms. We had built few friendly ties with other Christian groups and had thrashed and alienated them. Many of our pastors had sermons that they could no longer honestly preach.

For the past forty years we have been trying to rebuild our theological foundations on firmer ground. No one yet has been able to come up with a substitute which places the movement in a place of such exclusiveness and uniqueness that it elevates us above and beyond all other believers. It is doubtful that any one will. James and John played this dangerous game when they came to Jesus asking for a special position in the kingdom. Jesus rebuked them by asking if they could "drink of my cup?" We are not called to exercise a "most favored nation" status. Our mission is hardly to come forward with an irrefutable argument that of all believers, we enjoy a special status with the Almighty. Rather, we must accept the pain and embarrassment of our frustration with humility before the Lord and lay again those great, supporting, biblical timbers that will support the true Temple of God.

Marks of Greatness

Now looking back over this past half-century, what are the marks of greatness which emerge in our movement? Do we have any great stars left in the sky? Yes! I shall touch briefly on a few.

1. *The Centrality of Christ.* Warner and our pioneers had a high Christology. Christ was savior, Christ was healer, Christ was Lord and guide, Christ was teacher, Christ was head of the Church. We may smile at many of the strange ways in which this came to be expressed, but one can never honestly search the record and come up with any other conclusion than that our forefathers had a deep, relentless, searching hunger after Christ and a profound commitment to be like him in spirit and conduct. This expressed itself in earnest prayer, constant study of the life of Christ, and the most humbling expressions of dedication I have ever known. Warner wrote these lines:

O Christ, I can but love the; What heart could e'er withold
A love that cost so dearly The off'ring of thy soul? O King
of love immortal, Reign in my heart alone, And flood this
earthen temple With glory from thy throne. Amen.

Of such centrality is born the most spiritually sensitive
and Christlike people. Through the years we have had
many.

2. *People of the Covenant.* Central also in early Church of
God teaching was the biblical concept that God has acted
in history to bring into being a people, called by his
name, through whom he was going to attempt in a
special way to do his redemptive work. This ancient
article of faith, born in the time of Abraham and fulfilled
in the commissioning of the early church, is as valid
today as it has ever been. It is this ancient root system
that anchors our movement into the vast, universal,
catholic church. It is here, rather than in any prophetic
scheme, that we discover today who and what we are
and what our mission is to be.

3. *Freedom from sectarian bondage.* There was the strong
ring of truth in our early preaching that called for the
redeemed to renounce every vestage of sectishness and
step out into a life of freedom to join heart and hand with
every child of God on the face of the earth. Seen against
the shameful denominational quarreling and bickering of
the 1880s and the high creedal and organizational walls of
the times, this was an exciting and exhilarating stand to
take. Naylor, our foremost doctrinal songwriter, wrote:

The Church that was built when Pentecost came, The
Church that is kept in one faith and one Name, Shall
shine on resplendent, forever the same; I'll never go back,
I'll never go back.

This membership in the great family of God through the
new birth, standing in Christ alone, reaching hands in
fellowship to every blood-washed one, is still a powerful,

The College and Gospel Trumpet community looked like this before World War II. Old Main is at left; the publishing plant, center right; campgrounds, upper left.

scriptural, and compelling idea. We have existed now for nearly a hundred years without church joining and its false securities. The idea is sound and needs to be shared.

4. *Spontaneity*. Although there was a great deal of freewheeling in the early days in our common worship, still there was a refreshing spontaneity and excitement. Church was where the action was: testimonies to salvation, witnesses to miraculous healing, ringing songs of victory, powerful and stirring preaching, lives being saved and transformed. When it went to excess—as J. A. Morrison used to say, "whopping it up"—it was a disgrace. At their best, however, these services were a powerful relief from the crusty, deal, formal, rituals that were standard fare in most denominations. It would be great to recapture it at its best.

5. *Central place of the Word*. The pioneers were first, last, and always students of the Bible. It was the written *Word* that gave authority; the *Word* that was the vehicle of the light; the *Word* that spoke to the kind of lives we were to lead; the *Word* which provided guidance, direction, and food for the soul. Fortunately, the movement never got caught up in the great fundamentalist controversies that rocked the religious world early in the century. Nonetheless, a part of our greatness in the past has been derived from a diligent study of the Word. No renewal of the life of our movement will come any other way. Topical preaching has had its day. A new generation is coming on with a hunger to read and know the Scriptures. It would be tragic for us—with such a heritage—to be unaware of it.

6. *A deep and relentless hunger for the presence and power of the Holy Spirit*. I have spoken earlier of some of our excesses in handling the biblical doctrine of sanctification. This beautiful gift to believers sets their life apart for the Lord, strengthens and empowers them for service, assures them of the undergirding presence of the Holy Spirit, and purifies their inner being. It is one of the

Severely crippled much of his life, Charles Naylor engaged in a significant ministry of writing from his home.

great treasures of the Church of Jesus Christ. Rightly and sanely understood it bears witness to one of the timeless hungers of humanity—the yearning after holiness. Naylor wrote these tender lines:

Spirit holy in me dwelling,
Ever work as thou shalt choose;
All my ransomed pow'rs and talents
For thy purpose thou shalt use.

O how sweet is thy abiding!
O how tender is the love
Thou dost shed abroad within me
From the Father-heart above!

Thou hast cleansed me for thy temple,
Garnished with thy graces rare;
All my soul thou art enriching
By thy fullness dwelling there.

In me now reveal thy glory,
Let thy might be ever shown;
Keep me from the world's defilement,
Sacred for thyself alone.

REFRAIN

Spirit holy, Spirit holy,
All my being now possess;
Lead me, rule me, work within me,
Through my life thy will express. Amen.

7. *Richness of inspired hymns and spiritual songs.* One of
the great legacies of our movement is our treasury of
songs. The entire theology of the Church of God could be
reconstructed from such songbooks as *Reformation Glory.*
A whole cadre of songwriters made their appearance in
the first twenty-five years. Warner, Byers, Teasley,
Warren, and Naylor flooded the publishing company
with exciting music. One of the most attractive features of
our early work was the singing. Accompanying most
evangelists was a troupe of singers who sang
enthusiastically in railroad stations, street corners,
homes, schoolhouses, and nearly anywhere. It was
ringing, boistrous music, and it attracted and inspired
people everywhere. Dozens of songbooks came off our
presses. Anderson College is gratified to note that its
distinguished vice president and dean, Robert Nicholson,
has refined and edited the last two hymnals of the
Church of God. Who will ever forget these great first
lines:

"There's a mighty reformation sweeping o'er the
    land."
"Hark! my soul, seraphic music. . . ."
"Our Father's wondrous work we see. . . ."

93

"How sweet this bond of perfectness,
  The wonderous love of Jesus. . . ."
"Since Jesus gave his life for me
  Should I not give him mine?"
"I will praise the Lord who bought me, hallelujah!"
"Whether I live or die, Whether I wake or sleep,
  . . . I am the Lord's, I know."

8. *A clear, authentic vision of the Church.* This vision of the people of God which fired Warner and his associates asked for a "called out" community of the firstborn, the entire congregation of the redeemed, with Christ as the head, the door, the energizer, the organizer, the Lord who sets the members in the Body distributing gifts and callings through his wisdom. Through the years this biblical view of the Church has held solid as the Rock of Gibraltar and its truth has not been shaken. It is the only basis upon which true unity between Christians can come. We need not fear that such a foundation will erode with the passage of time.

9. *A global vision.* From the earliest days our leaders saw theirs as a global mission, one destined in Riggle's familiar phrase to "encircle the globe." Something dynamic and exciting had broken into their time, and their vision was to get the message out to the whole world. It was to this task that the presses at Gospel Trumpet Company were dedicated as they turned out tons of Christian literature that found its way into country after country around the world. This vision of great adventures and victories for God challenged the pioneers to new and creative methods of evangelism and outreach. It was carried forward with loyalty and devotion. It captured the imagination. It engendered boundless enthusiasm which swept aside the little currents of extremism, and brought the saints to their feet at camp meeting singing, "There's a mighty reformation sweeping o'er the land" and "I'm on the winning side."

Each age is a dream that is dying
or one that is coming to birth.

—Arthur O'Shaughnessy (1844-81)

The eternal God is at work in this universe and on our planet. The great Designer's hand in our affairs may not always be apparent, and his ways are often wrapped in unfathomable mystery. What is apparent, however, is that growth and decay are a part of the scheme of things. That is, always there are things dying and things being born—ideas, people, systems, plants—in our amazing total ecological system which is the dynamic environment in which each of us lives.

Candidates for the ministry are ordained in a service in the 1940s. Participants include (from left) J. A. Morrison, C. E. Brown, Earl Martin, Adam Miller, and E. A. Reardon. The work of the church moves on to the future.

In this setting we see God the Creator still at work, to shape and fashion all of life according to his plan. It is against this majestic scene that we come to understand the meaning of the last reformation.

The adjective *last* has validity only if it is thought of in terms of a continuing creative thrust of God's energy into the world. If a group is a part of this divine thrust—if they are self-committed to be used by him, if they have become spiritually reborn and sensitized to his will and active in his service—then wherever they are or by whatever name they are called they are part of the last reformation.

It is time to ring again this great reformation bell. The centennial is no time to cast a quick, curious eye on the past or to study our history as a movement from a detached cultural perspective. It is time to look long and hard at those great pillars of fire in our night which lit the way for our fathers. It is time to discard the old wineskins that can never take the sweet new wine of truth. It is time to break free from every trap set for us by the enemy and to climb out of every pit into which we have fallen. It could be that God is calling us out of our past, watching to see if there really is a people worthy of his covenant today. With these he would work to carry forward his creative, redemptive mission in the world. I believe it is true and I want us passionately to be a part of it.

On the site of Old Main at Anderson College today stands Decker Hall, the school's administration building.